Sc

Encouraging Small Families
Restricting U.S. tax exemptions to two children per family (though not taking exemptions away from children who already have them) will send a needed message to ourselves and to the world that we are encouraging small families.

Infant and Child Mortality
Support the work of mortality reduction for its own sake, but not in the hope that it will reduce the world population growth rate. It won't.

Loving Our Children
Our major concern should be for the children who are already here. We can provide best for them both by insisting that society devotes ample resources for their care and also by limiting future births. A society that assumes the obligation to provide adequately for its children also has the right to say how many shall be born.

A Child's Fundamental Right
A child has the right not to be born unless assured of health, education, opportunity, nutrition and a secure home with loving mother and father.

Consumption and World Population
Our excessive and wasteful consumption of energy and natural resources must be greatly reduced if we are to succeed in persuading poorer countries to lower their fertility.

Women's Rights
Men can no longer deprive women of a full voice in reproductive decisions, and must also respect women's equality in the economic and political world.

Male Responsibility

Men should assume major responsibility in birth control and spare women from having to resort to harmful methods. The condom is possibly as good a contraceptive as we will ever need or have.

Abortion

The real abortion issue is whether women may be compelled to bear children against their will. The way to prevent abortions is to prevent unwanted pregnancies by contraception and sexual responsibility.

Sex

Unwed childbearing is disastrous to our children. It is less due to male joblessness than to easy and irresponsible sex. Our obsession with sex is also causing divorce, rape, and child abuse, and keeping the poor from rising out of poverty. It's time to discourage sex stimuli in the media and adopt a higher standard of sexual responsibility.

Population Growth

The annual excess of births over deaths in the developing countries is at least 86 million, and is the main factor forcing population movements. Europe's annual excess of births over deaths a century ago was only about 5 million.

Immigration

A nation has the sovereign right to restrict immigration and to enforce its restrictions, for protection of its own people and fairness to those persons seeking to immigrate legally. Nations with high population growth must curb that growth rather than calling on other nations to absorb it.

Refugees

Displacement of people must be prevented by stopping famine, conflict, despotism, wherever they occur, supplying food, using population and development assistance, and armed force if needed. Refugee privileges must no longer be abused to circumvent immigration restrictions or encourage mass migration.

World Population Growth

George E. Immerwahr

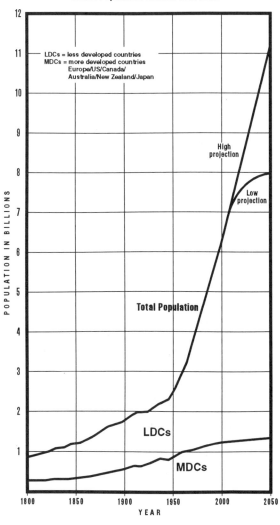

World Population Growth 1800-2050

LDCs = less developed countries
MDCs = more developed countries
Europe/US/Canada/
Australia/New Zealand/Japan

High projection

Low projection

Total Population

LDCs

MDCs

POPULATION IN BILLIONS

YEAR

During the 50 years following the year 2000, population of less developed countries could increase by as little as 1.5 billion or as much as 5 billion. Population of more developed countries will grow only slightly by natural increase, but could grow substantially by immigration from less developed countries.

PEANUT BUTTER
PUBLISHING

ISBN # 0-89716-552-7
11.5015

Cover design: David Marty Designs
Editor: Mike Brennan
Production: Elizabeth Lake

First printing January 1995

10 9 8 7 6 5 4 3 2 1

Peanut Butter Publishing
226 2nd Avenue West
Seattle, WA 98119

Table of Contents

Dedication

To the world's children, in the hope
that they'll treat this world
better than their parents did.

A Post-Election Note

The November 1994 American election results shifting power to the political right may bear results that will disappoint all those who share the feelings expressed in this book. On world population matters, the newly elected Congress may take much less interest and commit much less money than was hoped for by the U. S. delegation to the Cairo population conference.

American children may be adversely affected by cutbacks in Head Start and in educational programs generally, and by lack of progress in health programs. The "Contract with America" proposal for children's tax credits may be similar in form (but not in amount) to that of the National Commission on Children described in Chapter 4 of this book. It is unlikely, however, to operate in the manner described in Chapter 19, which would discourage large families by excluding credits for future-born children where there are already two or more in the family.

The newly elected Congress will obviously be unsympathetic to the tax ideas expressed in Chapter 18. Instead, its "middle-class tax cut" may take the same form as the Reaganomics tax-rate reductions which produced far greater increases in after-tax income for the wealthiest families than for middle-class.

The new Congress may not succeed in its attempts to erode abortion rights. But its ideas on welfare reform, combined with its support of the Hyde Amendment prohibition of abortion-funding, may result in many poor women bearing children for whom no AFDC benefits whatsoever will be available.

These reversals may themselves be reversed by the 1996 elections.

The passage of Initiative 187 in California, even if it is invalidated by the courts, has sent an angry message on illegal immigration both to the Mexican people and government and to our own federal government. Even though NAFTA was passed without any agreement by the Mexican government to discourage the flow of illegal immigrants, there may now be new and strong actions on both federal legislative and diplomatic fronts.

Explanation of Some Abbreviations and Terms Used in this Book

MDC
More developed country. The MDCs are the United States, Canada, Japan, Australia, New Zealand, and all European countries.

LDC
Less developed country. The LDCs are all countries not listed as MDCs, and include all the countries of Latin America and the Caribbean, Africa, and Asia other than Japan.

UN or U.N.
United Nations

Fertility
A rate of childbearing which relates the annual number of births to number of women of childbearing age.

Birth rate
A rate which relates number of births to the entire population. A country's crude birth rate is the number of births in a year divided by the country's total population averaged over the course of the year (or the population as of July 1 of that year). The crude birth rate is usually expressed per 1,000 of population.

Mortality
A rate which relates the annual number of deaths of persons of a given age to the number of persons of that age. See the Demographic Appendix for further details.

Death rate
Analogous to birth rate

Life expectancy at birth
The average number of years of expected lifetime of a newborn child. See Demographic Appendix for method of calculation.

Preface

How would you like to live in a world with twice as many people as it has today?

If you're now over 40, you may not live to see that happen since experts predict it will not be until about the year 2050 that world population can reach 11 billion, about twice its present size. But most of today's young children may still be living in 2050.

To many, the prospect of a world with 11 billion people is frightening. It would include the prospects of starvation, of further degradation of the environment, of civil tensions and of wars.

These population-related problems first became apparent around 1950 when the world's annual population growth rate rose sharply from about 1 percent to almost 2 percent. Since 1950, people in many countries have been studying the problem, and much has been done to slow the growth rate in the hopes that world population would peak before reaching 8 billion. Several international conferences addressed the problem, the most recent in September 1994 in Cairo, Egypt.

The problem of population growth had engaged my interest for several years prior to my living and working in what were then called Third World countries. I had read books about India and many other undeveloped countries and was appalled by the conditions of poverty and disease there. I thought if poverty and disease could be obliterated, people would have smaller families and population growth would soon come to a halt. Many people still think so, both in the developing and developed worlds.

The problem as I see it now is this: How do people regard the function of children, and what is their purpose in having them?

World Population Growth

I do not question the fact that people everywhere love their children, but they may not all love them intelligently. We are told that parents have many children because they will need sons for support in old age. We are also told that, because of high infant and child death rates, parents purposely have extra children to make up for children who may die. In this book, I admit these may be the reasons that motivate many parents, particularly in the developing world.

But I note first that, for the most part, these reasons are no longer valid. I also raise this question: To the extent that people have children because they really want them, and not simply because they have had sex, do they carefully consider the children's future welfare? Do people love children to such an extent that they will decide not to have a child unless there is a reasonable prospect the child's life will be happy and secure and will bless not only the parents, but the child itself? My contention is that if more people really did this, far fewer children would be born.

Every year there are many new and excellent books written on population, but most of them are written by scholars. Unfortunately it is mostly scholars that read them. I agree with most, but not all, of what they write.

I share the view that the excessive consumption of natural resources, of which we in the advanced countries are guilty, is at least as disastrous as the population growth in the developing countries. I also agree with the great need for the empowerment of women in today's world. We men have tried to manage the world for centuries, and we have grossly mismanaged it.

The world's salvation may really lie with the 1.9 billion children who are now under age 15 and who will become potential parents themselves over the next 15 years. If all of them can be educated and motivated to have only two children themselves, their future and the future of their children will be much brighter than appears today. In the meantime, we must do much more than we do for these children.

Since I urge couples not to have more than two children, you may ask why my wife and I had three. Our three sons were born years ago (the youngest will soon be 50). I suppose we might have stopped with a second child had that child been a daughter. In the book, I tell how Asian families with a number of daughters

Preface

keep on having children in the hope that they will have at least as many sons. Our situation was the reverse of theirs.

There are many people whom I should like to thank for what I have learned from them. First of all, the faculty and graduate students at the Center for Demography and Ecology at the University of Washington. Also the faculties of several other population study centers where I have worked and studied over the years. But I have learned most from students and other individuals in the overseas countries where I have worked.

The opinions expressed in this book, however, are my own, and I realize that some of them depart from the views held by many authorities on population.

An earlier version of this book was written in 1991, but no attempt was made to publish it. Several people who read portions of it gave me valuable comments, which helped me in the preparation of this book. They are too numerous to name, but I express my gratitude to them.

Elliott Wolf of the Peanut Butter Publishing Company in Seattle was enough interested in my population concerns to encourage me to prepare this version for publication. He recommended I take advantage of the editorial assistance offered by Mike Brennan of Pacific Rim News Service. Mike worked patiently with me, trying to help me whip my ideas into shape. I'm grateful to both Mike and Elliott, but if you still can't follow what I'm trying to say, blame me, not them.

Above all, I thank my wife Jean who has been my companion and greatest help for well over half a century. She shared my life and experience overseas, and also wrote for publication on India's population and related matters. I also thank her for her ever-loving patience while I was writing this book.

I've tried to write a non-scholarly and simple book, one that doesn't have reference notes, though it does have an appendix that should help you understand the quantitative aspects of population. Most of the figures in the book are drawn from publications of the Population Reference Bureau of Washington, D.C., or are my own estimates. If you have questions, send them to me through the publisher, and I may be able to answer them.

George Immerwahr
October 1994

Chapter 1

Introduction

This book has several purposes. The first is to describe and explain, in numerical terms, the rapid growth of world population that has taken place since about 1950. Even before 1950, the human population had grown over many centuries, but the annual growth rates of the past were far less than the growth rate since 1950.

Another purpose will be to describe some of the disturbing consequences of recent population growth and of the expected growth of the next several decades. You have already read much about these consequences, such as environmental degradation and possible food shortages, and I will try not to repeat too much of what you have read and heard. I will deal more with other concerns, such as overcrowding and civil and political tensions and the movement of peoples. And I will refer particularly to the plight of the world's children.

Population conferences

Still another purpose will be to report on the international population conferences in which these issues have been discussed.

The International Conference on Population and Development scheduled for September 1994 has now taken place in Cairo, Egypt. I will refer in this book to the objectives of the

Conference. One major objective is to slow the current rate of population growth, in the hope that the world's population in 2015 will not exceed 7.1 billion, which is the lowest of the various projections made for that year by United Nations demographers. The estimated population in mid-1994 was 5.6 billion. If the 7.1 billion limit is not to be exceeded, the average annual population growth over the next 21 years cannot exceed 72 million. The current annual growth is at least 90 million.

But the concerns of the Conference planners were not limited to population numbers. The Conference Document dealt also with the world's environment, with the reduction of poverty, with the status of women and their reproductive rights, with health and survival, and with "sustainable development." By sustainable development is meant the type of development that can improve the present economy without endangering the environment of the future. The Document also described the amounts of money which will be required to fund population and development assistance, and it expressed these in terms of GNP percentages. Developing nations themselves are to bear a major share of these costs.

The first several days of the Conference were taken up with arguments about abortion, to which reference will be made in a later chapter. This issue was finally resolved with compromise language, but insufficient time was left for full discussion of other issues. While the Conference concluded with a general consensus, it must be remembered that the final provisions of the Conference Document are not binding on the 180 individual nations that participated. All we can say is that the Conference received enough publicity that its findings and recommendations will be well remembered.

The two previous world population conferences had much less consensus. In the 1974 conference, the advanced countries, led by the United States, urged reduction of population growth through the greater use of contraception in the developing countries. But the developing countries insisted that underdevelopment and unfair world economic policies, and not population growth, were their real concerns. Their slogan was: "Development is the best contraceptive."

At the 1984 conference, developing countries acknowledged that population growth was a problem and asked for more

Introduction

help to enable them to curb it. But this time it was the United States that was "neutral" on population, and actually opposed any population growth reduction measures that even tolerated abortion.

The condition of the world's children

I have mentioned my concern for the plight of the world's children. I hope you love children as I do. I am thrilled every time I see the smile of a baby or small child, or hear a small child's happy, piping voice. Whenever this happens, I like to think that the child's joy and innocence will continue forever, even into those years when he or she will be immersed in the serious and responsible activities of adulthood.

That is why I am so distressed when I see children living in the miserable conditions I have so often seen both in the developing countries where I have lived and worked, and also in the United States. At night on Latin American city streets, I have often seen small children, sometimes two or three huddled up together in a single blanket, children abandoned by mothers unable to provide for them. In India I have seen great numbers of child beggars; a small child will hold out one hand to take your money and show you that the other hand was cut off to make him a more appealing beggar. In American inner cities and in Appalachia, I have seen families in unbelievably wretched conditions, one composed of a single mother with nine children all of whom looked to be within a 10-year age span.

But worst of all are the conditions of the children in the many troubled areas in Africa. Rwanda is the area of most recent concern, but tragic events took place in Somalia and Ethiopia just a short time ago. The media have not featured conditions in other troubled African countries such as Mozambique or Angola, but we may hear more about these areas soon.

There's no need to show pictures of distressed children in this book. Just look at television or the newspapers, and you'll see scenes of human tragedy at its worst. Look especially at the pictures of the starving and refugee children in Africa. And you can see in the pictures something the media seldom tell you in words: that these are mainly the children of parents who had too many; of societies that had too many.

World Population Growth

What the media won't tell you

For somehow, the media, and even the children's advocates, don't want to talk about the overpopulation of nations or of families. Or to talk about population density or population growth. When you read the accounts of the Haitian boat people, or saw their pictures, were you told that Haiti is a country with 700 people per square mile, and has become almost completely deforested because of its population growth? A description of Haiti by Jacques-Yves Cousteau is given in a later chapter of this book. When pictures of Rwandans were on television and in every newspaper, did you learn that the population density of Rwanda was over 800 per square mile? The U.S. density is only 84 if you don't include Alaska, which would dilute it to 74.

Not that you should evaluate a country's conditions merely on the basis of population density. Japan also has a population density of over 800 persons per square mile. But Japan's rural and non-mountainous areas have a mean density far below Rwanda's, since Rwanda is almost wholly rural. Moreover, Japan has virtually no population growth. Japan has a great industrial base which keeps its people active and affluent. Japan has a highly disciplined and an ethnically homogeneous population. Japan's children under age 18, whom society must feed and educate, are only 21 percent of its population, while in Rwanda children under 18 are at least 50 percent.

You might not agree with me that the crises of Rwanda and Haiti are related to their crowded conditions. But wouldn't you at least agree that higher population density certainly means more casualties when crisis strikes? You may not believe that a country's rapid population growth has contributed to starvation. But wouldn't you at least admit that it's harder to relieve hunger in Somalia's present population of 10 million than it would have been if the population had remained at its earlier size of 6 million?

There are many problems in the world that have an unrecognized population growth factor. Where, for example, can displaced people be resettled, when their number has rapidly grown and when there are so few under populated places that might serve for refuge? The Palestinians who were displaced in 1948 are a case in point. They demand to be resettled in their original homeland, but their number has probably doubled or even tripled over the past 46 years. Meanwhile, that former homeland has also greatly grown in population, due to immigration of Jews from Europe and from other Arab lands.

Even when problems in the United States are reported, the full population facts and the important numbers are not given and sometimes not even asked, as you will read in later chapters.

How the developing countries view population growth

The most rapid population growth since 1950 has been in the developing countries of Asia, Africa and Latin America. This growth has not been the result of an increase in human fertility (births), but instead the result of the great reduction in human mortality (deaths) which has taken place since the close of World War II. Certainly none of us would want a return to the higher mortality of the past. The solution to the problem of population growth must therefore involve reducing fertility to a level close to the greatly reduced level of mortality.

I worked in family planning and related fields for a total of 10 years in South Asian countries, and periods of a few months each in African and Latin American countries. In the course of my work, I made the following observations about people's views on population growth and overpopulation:

1. Even though many people recognized that rapid population growth was taking place and was causing problems, they were unaware of the reduction in mortality that had taken place. They also did not view high birth rates or large family size as contributing to their problems. When I was in India, the preferred family size was four children — not merely four born, but four surviving to adulthood. A population with average families that size would double in a generation. In much of Africa the preferred size is still six children.

2. Even though many people did view population growth as a problem, others viewed population growth as desirable. Some were strongly nationalistic and believed that growth would make their country stronger than neighboring countries. Others claimed that more hands were needed for economic development

3. Some people felt the solution to overpopulation was emigration to a less populated country. For people in India, the country of choice was either the United States, Great Britain or

Australia. The immigration restrictions of these countries were deeply resented.

4. Whether people had consciously planned to have several children for their own economic security, or had children simply because they had sex, they gave little thought to what the future welfare of their children might be.

It was this last observation which particularly distressed me. I do not condemn people for this lack of concern; each generation has just taken it for granted that their children would make out somehow, just as they had made out themselves. But I became convinced that if people did give thoughtful consideration to the future welfare of their children, taking into account the conditions of these times, far fewer children would be born.

Other topics

There has also been considerable population growth in the advanced countries of Europe, North America and Australia in this century, though the recent growth rate has been less than in the developing countries. In this book, I will discuss the nature of this population growth also, and the factors contributing to it.

Still other topics will include the status of women — a most important subject at the Cairo Conference — and the various behavioral, cultural and religious factors entering into the population equation. Concern for the world's children will be a factor entering the discussion of almost every topic.

How attainable is the Conference goal?

If world population growth can be slowed so as not to exceed 7.1 billion by 2015, then there would also be some hope that world population could level off before reaching 8 billion.

To me, a world population no greater than 7.1 billion in 2015 seems highly improbable but not impossible. To attain that goal would require a marked reduction in the average number of births per woman, particularly in the LDCs (the less developed countries in Asia, Africa and Latin America). Such a reduction would be difficult even if the LDCs had stable economies and peaceful internal and external political relationships. Instead, the world is faced with drastic problems such as national and ethnic conflicts, terrorism, famines, despotic oppression, even threats of nuclear war. Even though these problems are population-related, priorities will naturally be given to direct solution of the short-term effects, rather than to the underlying longer-term population growth problem.

Moreover, reducing the number of births per woman will require marked changes in life styles and mentality. Better education and an improved social status of women can be expected to relieve women of some of the excessive fertility that now burdens them. But on the other hand, women themselves often attach a high value to having large families, and many will be unwilling to give up the security of having a number of sons.

The main agenda of this book will be the welfare of children, a topic which is usually subordinated to that of the welfare of parents. Even in the United States, too many children are conceived and born with little or no thought to their future welfare. An entire chapter will be devoted to American sexuality and childbearing, and will point out the danger of the perpetuation of an impoverished underclass.

Still another chapter will tell how our own population growth rate is kept high by immigration and the high fertility of immigrants. It raises the question as to how much of other countries' population growth we are morally obligated to absorb.

The desired slowing of population growth will require great sacrifice. Peoples in the less developed countries will have to abandon many traditional values, including their present ideas that they must have large families. They will have to agree to fuller societal and familial roles for women, and families will have to forego their preference for sons.

But the developing countries will not agree to such sacrifice unless we of the developed world make substantial sacrifices of a different nature. Even though we of the advanced countries are only one-fifth of the world's population, we consume the major share of the earth's scarcest resources. We are the people whose life styles are the major causes of pollution of the environment. We are the people who have the richest diet. We are the people who profit from the manufacture of weapons used both in the developing nations and by ourselves. We Americans are the people who insist on driving our own cars instead of using public transportation.

World Population Growth

If the United States is to exercise world leadership in the solution of world population and development problems, we Americans must takes steps to show developing countries that we are willing to match their sacrifices. Even the transfer of wealth to the developing countries will not be enough. Even though our own fertility is no higher than replacement level, we must take steps to make it even lower.

I will discuss some of the needed steps in later chapters, and particularly in the final chapter of this book. These steps may be just a beginning of what we will have to do.

Chapter 2

World Population Growth

*"The great demographic transition came when
death rates fell"*
— Ansley J. Coale, Princeton University

Picture the northeastern United States, an area bounded
by the Mississippi River to the west and by the Ohio River and
Mason-Dixon Line to the south. An area that contains the old
industrial centers of the eastern seaboard and the Great Lakes.
An area that's home to 94 million people, more than one-third of
the U.S. population.

Why is this area and its population of interest? Because in
each year for the rest of this century, the worldwide population
growth will be about enough to repopulate the northeastern United
States. In 1994 alone, 141 million people will have been born and
51 million will have died, a net gain of 90 million people. In the
year 2000, the annual gain may near 100 million people.

During the 19th century the world's population almost
doubled, growing from 0.8 billion to over 1.5 billion. In this century it will have almost quadrupled, passing 6 billion by the year
2000.

Births and deaths

Why this acceleration in world population growth? Are
birth rates rising? No. In fact, in most parts of the world they are
falling. But death rates have been falling much faster. When the
20th century began, more than 120 of every 1,000 babies born in

9

the United States could be expected to die before reaching their first birthday. In 1990, 9 out of 1,000 infants died (8.3 in 1993).

In 1900, only about 75 percent of babies born in the United States could be expected to survive to age 20; today the survival rate is 98 percent. In 1900, the "life expectancy at birth" — the average number of years of expected lifetime — was just under 50. Today it averages 72 years for newborn boys, 79 for new born girls. In Europe, there have been survival gains similar to ours.

In the less developed countries of Latin America, Asia and Africa (we will use the term LDCs to mean less developed countries and MDCs to mean the more developed), the gains in survival are relatively greater than ours, even though their mortality is higher than ours. In Mexico, life expectancy at birth improved from about 30 in 1900 to about 70 now. In India it improved from about 25 in 1900 to about 57 now.

Death rates in Europe fell steadily in the 1800s. One reason was improved nutrition, which in turn was the result of economic advancement, brought about by more efficient production and distribution of food. Survival also improved through public health measures such as better sanitation and provision of potable water. Improved education brought about better personal hygiene and child care. Smallpox was virtually wiped out by vaccination. The use of medicines played a relatively minor role.

In the developing countries, however, few of these advances came about until well into this century, but when they did come, their effects were rapid. Immunization and the reduction of endemic diseases played a more important role in the LDCs than in Europe or the United States.

Fertility is often measured in terms of the total fertility rate (TFR), the average number of children a woman bears if she lives to age 50. In most European countries TFR is in the range of 1.3 to 2. In the United States TFR is currently about 2, but varies for different ethnic groups, being below 2 for non-Hispanic whites and Asians, above 2 for blacks and Hispanics. In most LDCs TFR was over 6 earlier in this century, but it is now below 4 in Mexico and in India, over 6 in much of Africa, below 3 in most of the Caribbean countries, except in Haiti where it is still 6.

What You Should Know

The demographic transition

Deaths and births are also measured in terms of what are called *crude* death and birth rates, the number of deaths (or births) in a year per 1,000 of population. The transition over time from high to low death rates and from high to low birth rates is called the "demographic transition." The accompanying chart illustrates how this transition differed as between Europe and the developing world.

Because of the high proportion of young people, crude death rates in some LDCs are now lower than those in Europe. In Europe death rates were already declining well before 1700. Birth rates in Europe started declining around 1850 and by now are practically no higher than death rates. In the meantime, however, birth rates were well in excess of death rates. The excess of birth over death rates is the "natural increase rate", which in Europe never exceeded 15 per 1,000, or 1.5 percent. Birth rates fell after death rates fell, but not necessarily because death rates fell. This issue will be discussed later.

In the LDCs by contrast, death rates hardly declined until this century, but by 1950 were declining very rapidly, while birth rates had hardly begun to decline. The result has been a natural increase rate of 23 per 1,000 (2.3 percent) on average in the LDCs and as high as 3 percent in some of these countries.

While 2.3 or 3 percent may seem a very low rate of annual growth, its compounding effect would surprise you. A population growing at 2.3 percent a year doubles in 30 years*, grows eight-fold in 90 years. In the 90 years between 1900 and 1990 Mexico's population grew six-fold, from 14 to 85 million, not counting the immigrants now in the United States, but the average annual growth percentage was only 2.0 percent.

In terms of absolute numbers, the excess of births over deaths in Europe seldom exceeded five million a year. About the year 1900, when this natural increase was at its peak, over a million Europeans a year were emigrating, primarily to the Americas, relieving Europe of much of the burden of population growth.

---

* Dividing the number 70 by the annual percentage of population growth will give the approximate number of years it takes for population to double. Here 70 divided by 2.3 is about 30. With 3.5 percent annual growth, doubling would be in 20 years.

11

World Population Growth

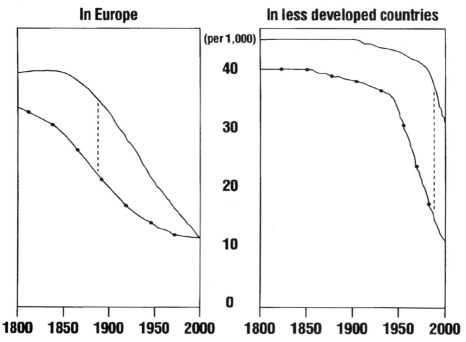

Typical Demographic Transitions
(short-term fluctuations not indicated)

In Europe   **In less developed countries**

(per 1,000)

40

30

20

10

0

1800 1850 1900 1950 2000   1800 1850 1900 1950 2000

Crude birth rate ——
Crude death rate —•—

Maximum
natural
increase

12

In stark contrast, today's LDC population is growing by 86 million a year, before emigration. For mass emigration to relieve LDC population woes, it would have to be a very large number indeed.

The movement of population

There is considerable population movement today among the LDCs of Asia, Africa or Latin America, and particularly within Africa as people flee from famines and tribal wars. There are also great numbers of people seeking to emigrate from the LDCs into Europe, North America and Australia.

Another great population movement is the migration of rural people to the cities. In 1900, perhaps no more than 14 percent of the world's people lived in cities with populations of 5,000 or more.

Today, about 50 percent do. More to the point, about 8 percent of the world's population live in cities of at least 5 million people. These mega-cities are found not only in major industrial countries, but also in the developing world. Tokyo-Yokohama, the world's highest populated urban area, is followed in order by Mexico City and Sao Paolo (the city in Brazil which few people had heard about 50 years ago). Among other mega-cities in the developing world are Bombay, Calcutta, Karachi, Cairo, Shanghai and Beijing.

A major reason for the rapid population growth of cities in Asia and Latin America, and to some extent in Africa, is that rural areas cannot absorb more than a fraction of their own population growth; agricultural areas cannot support many more people than they already have. But urban growth can't be blamed just on migration from the countryside. The annual excess of births over deaths in some cities is even greater than the annual number of migrants from rural areas. Even in these cities people have large families.

Cities today are having crucial problems, particularly in the LDCs, since it has been impossible to plan for or accommodate their population growth. Services such as sanitation, health care, disposal of garbage and waste, construction of housing and streets, public transportation, police protection, cannot begin to keep up with the numbers of people needing these services. More reference to these problems will be made in a later chapter.

World Population Growth

But despite flight to the cities, the population density of some rural areas is greater than most of us could possibly imagine. Bangladesh, a country smaller in area than the state of Iowa, has about 115 million people, compared with Iowa's 3 million. Some 100 million of these people live in villages, and the rural population density is about 1,800 people per square mile. Other places with great rural population densities include Vietnam, the islands of Java and Bali in Indonesia, Haiti and El Salvador, Rwanda and Burundi in central Africa, and various small island countries such as Barbados and Grenada.

Most of the population growth of the developing world has been since the close of World War II. It's been during this period that LDC death rates have so rapidly decreased. In the immediate future, the highest rates of population growth will be in sub-Saharan Africa. African death rates are declining substantially, despite AIDS, though they are still much higher than elsewhere in the world. African birth rates are declining only slowly.

As for future world population growth, we can only speculate. As mentioned earlier, it is hoped that the population in 2015 will have reached only 7.1 billion and will level off about the year 2050 before reaching 8 billion. However, the "best guess" among international demographers is that it will reach 8.5 billion in 2025 and continue growing well beyond that.

The United States, Canada and Australia will have continued population growth, but perhaps half of that would be by immigration from the LDCs. Europe's population may not grow at all except by immigration. Even today, its natural increase is virtually zero.

The age structure of population

So long as both birth rates and death rates remained high, the typical population consisted of a large proportion in the childhood ages, a moderate proportion at the working adult ages, and only a very small proportion of elderly people. Population composition is frequently portrayed by what is called a "population pyramid", in which the youngest members are represented by a layer at the bottom, and with successively older groups at higher levels. Males are usually shown at the left, females at the right.

What You Should Know

To illustrate, the pyramids representing the U.S. and Mexico populations in 1990 are shown in the first of two charts. The bottom layer represents children under age 5, with successively older 5-year age groups above. The U.S. representation is based on age and sex figures from the 1990 census, the Mexican on U.N. estimates. In this first chart the areas represent actual numbers. Since the population of Mexico was about one-third of the U.S. population, the areas are in strict proportions to the populations. In the second chart, however, the aim is to portray the difference in percentage distributions. Here the Mexican pyramid has the same total area as the U.S. pyramid, since each one represents 100 percent.

Note that as you go upward in each of the Mexico pyramids, each age group has distinctly fewer members than the next younger group. In Mexico each recent year's births has exceeded in number the previous year's, though there has been some slowing down over the last 15 years. In the United States, the births during the "baby boom" years 1946-64 were much more numerous than in years before or since, and the persons born in those years were at ages 25-44 in 1990.

Even though the 1990 population of Mexico was only one-third that of the U.S. population, Mexican children at ages 0-4 were almost two-thirds the number of U.S. children at that age. Since there is now very little difference in the mortality of the two countries, their relative numbers will stay more or less the same as the two sets of children grow up. This means that even if from now on fertility rates are the same in both countries, and if there were no emigration, the Mexican population would eventually be two-thirds of the U.S. population, rather than one-third. If Mexican fertility remains higher than ours, the Mexican population will overtake ours in a very few generations. The Mexican population was only 14 million in 1900, 26 million in 1950, 85 million in 1990. Were it not for emigration, the 1990 population would have been several million greater.

The second set of pyramids emphasizes the difference in age distributions. Note that in Mexico almost 40 percent of the 1990 population was under age 15, as compared to 22 percent for the United States. On the other hand, 13 percent of the U.S. population had reached age 65, as compared to 4 percent of the Mexican.

15

World Population Growth

1990 Populations of U.S. and Mexico

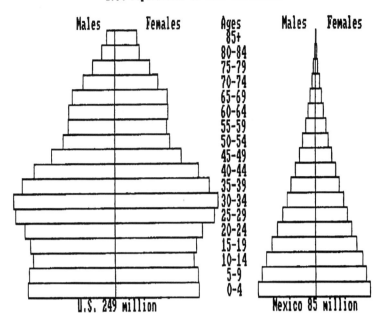

Age-Sex % Distributions of 1990 Populations

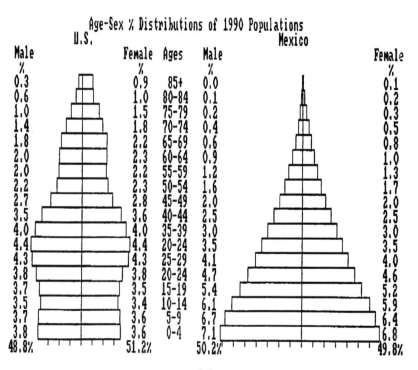

Note that in both populations males exceed females at birth, but by about age 45 females overtake males because of their higher survival. In a population with as high a percentage of older adults as the United States, females exceed males in the total population. In Mexico total males and total females are about equal, but in some LDCs males considerably outnumber females.

The aging of population

Only 6 percent of Americans were past their 65th birthday when the Social Security Act was passed in 1935. Today almost 13 percent are, and one-half of our population is past age 33. In some European countries, the percentages past age 65 are even higher than ours, 18 percent in Sweden, 16 percent in Britain. In most of Asia (except for Japan) and in Latin America the percentages of elderly are much lower. In Africa, where both fertility and mortality are very high, only 3 percent are past age 65.

But as both fertility and mortality fall, the percentages of elderly people will definitely rise, even in the LDCs. We in the United States have become aware of the increasing cost to provide social security, pensions and health care to elderly people as their proportion in the population rises. This poses a dilemma: We want to halt population growth, and yet don't know how to provide for the increasing proportion of elderly. This issue will be discussed later.

But the world's biggest problem is how to provide for all its children. Since children compete with each other for shares of the world's resources, we can help the children already here by holding down the number of births of new children.

Growth of the unemployed labor force

Even now, the proportion of young adults in LDC populations has grown, and to the point where their number has gone up much faster than jobs. Unemployment is particularly high among young adults in countries where much of the population is now urban. The working-age population of the LDCs is now rising by more than 60 million a year, and at least half of the labor-force entrants are unable to find even subsistence-level jobs. This is what is driving young adults to seek jobs in North America and Europe and affecting the job markets there. Western Europe is now facing the highest level of unemployment since World War II.

Society stresses the need for education, but the growth in the number of educated LDC young people is not matched by the growth in the number of jobs. Often it's a case of a mismatch between the skills supplied by schooling and the skills needed for employment. But sometimes it's a matter of a country's not having the economic development needed to utilize the education which the country has provided. In some countries, for example, many more young people have learned computer skills than the economy now needs, though such skills might be needed in the future.

While in our own country we find great numbers of unemployed young men who lack skills because they were school dropouts, LDCs are more likely to find that their young people who complete school have no jobs to enter. Or they may have cultures in which it is considered degrading for an educated young person to do physical or manual labor.

Still another current development is the growing number of women seeking paid employment. To the extent that women in the LDCs find paid work, fertility and population growth rates will decline, but meanwhile the unemployment problem will worsen.

It is likely that the world will never have full employment for all its citizens. Even now, there are men of all ages who can work but have never had full-time jobs. There will be great use of high skills to develop the advanced technology that will further automate production, but much reduced employment for those who lack these skills.

Population growth, by continent

The following table shows estimated population, in millions of persons, by continent, from 1800 to 1994, with the "best guess" projection for the year 2025. The figures for 1950 and earlier are from Carr-Saunders, those for 1994 and 2025 from the Population Reference Bureau. Estimates for the five Central Asian republics which were part of the Soviet Union are included in Asia rather than in Europe for all of the years shown.

What You Should Know

All of the current MDCs except Japan are included in the first set of sub-totals, which therefore understate the MDC totals. The second set of sub-totals slightly overstate the LDC totals.

	1800	1850	1900	1950	1994	2025
Europe (incl. Russia)	177	254	386	552	728	731
U.S. and Canada	6	26	81	166	290	375
Oceania	2	2	6	12	28	39
Sub-Total	185	282	473	730	1,046	1,145
Asia	532	683	874	1,410	3,392	5,017
Latin America & Carib.	19	33	63	164	470	679
Africa	100	100	141	220	700	1,538
Sub-Total	651	816	1,078	1,794	4,562	7,234
World Total	836	1,098	1,551	2,524	5,607	8,378

Population growth, past and future

Rulers of individual nations have ordered counts of their populations since long before the Christian era, but population estimates of the world or of individual continents for that period are very crude. It is estimated that the world population was about 250 or 300 million at the beginning of the Christian era, when Augustus ordered the census of the Roman Empire (see Luke 2:1). It probably reached 500 million about the year 1650. Population grew irregularly over the intervening centuries, and it sometimes decreased. During the 14th century, the bubonic plague — also called the Black Death — killed perhaps a quarter of the populations of Asia and Europe. The worldwide influenza epidemic of 1918-19 is believed to have killed over one percent of the world's population, including 500,000 Americans.

The world's future population growth depends largely on the degree by which fertility can be reduced. The above table shows an estimate for the year 2025 of about 8.4 billion, but this is only the middle of a number of estimates made by United Nations demographers. The farther into the future we go, the wider the range of estimates. One of the estimates for the year 2100 is 12.5 billion.

World Population Growth

*Our best hope is that all the world's children
now under age 15 can be educated to have
families of no more than two children*

There are right now about 1.9 billion children under age
15 in the world. Over the next 15 years they will have moved into
their reproductive ages. If infant and child mortality continue their
downward trend, the great majority of these children will still be
alive. The number of children they will have is the most important
factor affecting the world's future population. Should it become
possible to persuade them to have *on the average* only two children, rapid population growth will still continue for several decades, but an eventual end to population growth will be in sight.
If we can expect them to have a *maximum* of two children, the
world's TFR would fall to 1.7 or even lower, since some women
would have no children or only one. If that could happen, population would reach a peak within a much shorter period and eventually decrease.

So much depends on these children. The reproductive decisions they will make will be crucial. This is why girls and women
must have education at least equal to that of boys and men. This is
why education must emphasize the facts of population growth
and the need for male responsibility as well as female in fertility
control.

Will AIDS stop world population growth? Probably not,
but it has already slowed the growth. AIDS is the major cause of
death in several African countries, where its transmission is largely
heterosexual and where many deaths are those of children. The
above estimate of Africa's population in 2025, 1.5 billion,
takes estimated AIDS mortality into account. Were it not
for AIDS, Africa's population might reach 1.7 billion or more.

As will be discussed in a later chapter, infant and
child mortality are still very high in Africa, though in many
other LDCs they are now lower than ours were during the
1930s.

From now on, the greatest possible area for mortality reduction will be at the older adult ages, and it is likely that during
the 21st century the proportion of people surviving to and beyond
age 100 will be much higher than now. Just during the present
century there has been a marked advance in the survival to ages

What You Should Know

over 50. Today over one-half of all newborn American children have four grandparents still living; this would have been very rare a century ago. But the population growth effect of higher survival after the reproductive ages is relatively slight. Few people over 50 procreate children.

Some of the quantitative relationships mentioned in this chapter will be further explained in the Demographic Appendix of this book. This Appendix will also explain the "population momentum" which will cause the population of Mexico and other LDCs (and even of our own country) to continue to grow even if the TFR were to fall immediately to what is called "replacement level" or even well below that level.

Chapter 3

Human Fertility
Be fruitful, and multiply
— The Book of Genesis (1:28)

We've already noted that TFR, the total fertility rate, varies by country and also has varied over time. What is the range of fertility variation? What can be done to bring about fertility reduction?

The nature of fertility

Fertility is a rate of actual childbearing rather than a measure of ability to bear children. (The ability to bear a child is called "fecundity."* A woman who for health or other reasons is unable to bear a child is called infecund, or sterile.) A total fertility rate, TFR, is the mean total number of children born over a woman's reproductive years. It is usually calculated as the sum of the fertility rates for every age from 15 through 49. In any country or group, or at any period, TFR is of course an average, not the fertility of an individual woman.

The fertility of any individual woman depends on several factors. One factor, of course, is whether she has a male partner with whom she has sexual intercourse. Another is the regularity and frequency of intercourse. Another factor is the woman's fecundity; as already noted, some health problems may make a woman infecund, or make conception unlikely. Still another is

* The words in Spanish, French, etc., corresponding to the English words "fertility" and "fecundity" have meanings which seem more logical. The Spanish word "fertilitas" means the ability to bear a child, and "fecunditas" means the rate of actual childbearing.

her age, since conception can take place only during those ages when she would be menstruating, usually from age 12 or 13 to her late 40s. Fertility is higher at ages 18 through 30 than at younger or older ages. A woman is unlikely to conceive while she is fully breastfeeding a previously born child.

Also, she is unlikely to conceive if she is using efficient contraception. If she or her male partner has had a sterilization, she is extremely unlikely to conceive.

But even if all factors appear favorable for conception, a woman may still not conceive, or she may not conceive over a long interval. A woman who has been using contraception might conceive almost as soon as she stops its use. Or she may not conceive until many months later. Or she may never conceive.

Women of the Hutterite community, most of whose members live in north central and northwestern United States or adjacent parts of Canada, are believed to have higher fertility than that of any group in the world. Hutterite women reaching age 50 have given birth, on the average, to about 10 children. In other words, their TFR is approximately 10. Almost all Hutterites marry, their religion forbids contraception, and most babies are breast fed for only short periods. The Hutterite community is healthy and prosperous, so that conditions for high fertility are very favorable. Some demographers call Hutterite fertility "natural fertility", and use it as a yardstick in analysis of fertility of other groups.

Aside from the Hutterites, the highest TFRs are now in sub-Saharan Africa, where several individual countries have TFRs of 7.0 or higher. At the other extreme, Japan and several European countries have TFRs of 1.5 or lower.

Birth control

Do women, or couples, have the number of children they choose or plan to have, as many sociologists and anthropologists claim? Or do they have children merely because they have sex?

The answer must lie somewhere in between. Even in the United States, where birth control has been practiced for years, it is estimated that at least half of the pregnancies that occur areunplanned. In fact, many are definitely unwanted, as evidenced by the 1.5 million abortions that take place each year.

Human Fertility

As I have noted elsewhere, families prior to this century in both the United States and Europe were much larger than today, and this was not always because large families were wanted. There is ample evidence that British and American women despaired of frequent pregnancies and welcomed the work of birth control pioneers like Margaret Sanger. Women throughout history have been desperate to prevent or terminate unwanted pregnancies. Over the centuries abortion was the main method of controlling births. Infanticide was often used when abortion failed.

Men often were as aware as their wives of the problems of having too many children. In Europe, coitus interruptus, the withdrawal of the penis before ejaculation, was very common. It became so habitual that men still practiced it even after their wives began to use more modern birth control methods.

As the graphs in the preceding chapter show, the European birth rate was already declining by the mid-1800s; in France the decline began in the 1700s. Even before these declines, European fertility was well below the so-called natural fertility of the Hutterites. Forms of condoms and diaphragms somewhat similar to those used today were introduced in the mid-1800s, But cruder forms had been used much earlier. In the United States, birth control devices were barred from interstate commerce by a Federal law known as the Comstock Act. Some states also enacted anti-birth control laws. However, the prohibition of condoms was circumvented by representing them as prophylactics, packaging them with the instruction: "To be used for prevention of disease only."

State laws against abortion were enacted in the United States in the 1800s, and remained on the books in most states until the 1973 Supreme Court decision in Roe vs. Wade.

Delayed marriage of women

One situation that tends to reduce fertility is late marriage, since it shortens the period over which a woman can bear children. Since the likelihood of conception is usually at its peak before a woman reaches age 25, delay of marriage beyond that age may reduce fertility considerably.

In some societies, marriage for women has taken place at puberty or very shortly afterward. In India, it was once common for Hindu girls as young as five to go through marriage ceremonies, sometimes to boys not much older than themselves. The marriages were not consummated until puberty, but if in the meantime the groom were to die, the girl would be considered a widow and not be permitted to remarry. On the other hand, if the marriage were consummated at puberty, she might have successive pregnancies over a period of as many as 35 years, and possibly bear as many as 20 children.

In India and in some other countries of South and Southeast Asia, marriage is now much later than before. One such country is Sri Lanka, where many women are now not marrying until age 25 or later. This has been an important factor in reducing the Sri Lanka TFR to an estimated 2.5.

In most Muslim countries or communities, women still marry early. In Sri Lanka and India, where there are laws on minimum age of marriage, special exceptions for Muslims permit earlier marriage for women and multiple marriage for men. Multiple marriage is infrequent in both of these countries, but Muslim women do have higher fertility than women of other religions. In Arab countries as well, most women marry early and have relatively high fertility.

In countries where many women have babies before marriage, delay of marriage is of less importance. What is more important is the age of first sexual union.

Fertility and population growth

It should be easy to understand that the condition needed for a population not to decrease or to die out is for women on average to have at least two children surviving to an age when they themselves can become parents. If there are women who have no children or are unmarried and therefore do not have two surviving children, other women in the society will have to make up for them to bring the average to at least two.

When there are on average exactly two surviving children, the population will in the long run remain constant, but not necessarily in the short run. We call the situation of exactly two surviving children "replacement-level fertility" because the male children will replace fathers and female children will replace mothers. This is still the case even if some families have all boys or all girls, because some boys in all-boy families will replace fathers in all-girl families and girls in all-girl families will replace mothers in all-boy families.

Human Fertility

Having two surviving children per woman obviously requires an average slightly higher than two births per woman. This is because some children die before being adulthood, and because slightly less than half of all newborn babies are girls. Another factor, though of lesser importance, is the range of ages of women when their children are born.

Replacement-level fertility is currently about 2.1 in the United States, with slight variation between different races. But where infant and child mortality is much higher than ours, as in Africa, replacement-level fertility can be as high as 3.2. TFR in the United States is, for all races combined, though not for individual races, slightly lower than replacement-level. As the Demographic Appendix will show, the closeness of our TFR to replacement-level will mean that our population could stop growing early in the 21st century, if there is no net immigration.

The following table shows estimated TFRs and current estimates of replacement-level fertility for countries:

	Est. replacement-level fertility	Estimated TFR
United States	2.10	2.08
Mexico	2.22	3.34
Japan	2.09	1.50
Germany	2.10	1.35
Uganda	3.04	7.40

If one visualizes replacement-level fertility as the fertility needed to keep population stationary in the long run (assuming no net immigration), you can see that our population will stop growing in the long-run if fertility and mortality remain unchanged. Japan's and Germany's populations will decrease, Mexico's and Uganda's will increase, Uganda's very sharply. Detailed calculations for Mexico, as well as for the United States, will be shown in the Demographic Appendix.

It should be very clear that even though the mortality of countries like Uganda — or other countries in Africa — is much higher than ours, the claim that such a country needs its high fertility to compensate for its high mortality, is completely unfounded. A country like Uganda or Haiti (whose TFR is 6.0) could have fertility rates only half their present level and their populations would still grow.

World Population Growth

In no country of the world is it necessary to have an average of more than 3.2 births per woman in order to have the two surviving children needed to prevent population decrease.

Is having fertility at or below replacement-level a hardship? All European countries except Albania have fertility at replacement level or below (most of them well below). In Asia, Japan, China, Taiwan and South Korea have fertility below replacement level, and Thailand's is just at replacement level. In the Caribbean, Cuba and some smaller countries now have fertility below replacement level.

Fertility goals

The table on the preceding page compared TFRs with replacement-level fertility of several individual countries. It shows in effect that current U.S. fertility is closely equivalent to replacement level, that German and Japanese fertility levels are well below replacement and Ugandan far above it. National governments should know and understand how their own TFRs compare with replacement levels, so that they can formulate fertility goals and communicate these goals through the media and in the schools.

The Conference Document might have been more effective had it expressed fertility goals in terms of number of children per family

National governments are sometimes reluctant to do this, often because they feel that people will be offended. I remember how Sri Lanka schools taught population in terms of crude birth rates only (annual births per 1,000 population). Students might be told that the national birth rate was currently 30 per 1,000 (for example) but should be brought down to 25. During my years in Sri Lanka, I tried to tell the education authorities that rates like these meant little to students, that instead goals ought to be expressed in terms of numbers of children per family. The authorities were horrified at such an idea, because they felt that this would be a criticism of cultural norms and that students in large families would be ridiculed by those in small families.

Human Fertility

Such thinking may well have affected the drafters of the Conference Document. The Document contains many figures describing the rates and levels of present and projected future population growth, but it says almost nothing about fertility rates and their relation to replacement-level fertility. This may have been a weakness of the Document and possibly of the Conference itself. Setting specific goals in terms of fertility rates and family size, and then formulating policies to achieve these goals, should be the aim of individual countries. The Conference itself should have recommended this form of goal-setting. It should also have stressed the need for every country to aim toward or below the two-child norm.

Chapter 4

The World's Children and Their Rights

"A little child shall lead them"
— Isaiah (11:6)

Children in the developing world

There are almost 1.7 billion children under age 15 in the developing countries of Asia, Africa and Latin America, and great numbers of them live in peril of disease, starvation or violence. About 127 million LDC children will be born during 1994. Of these, 9 million will die before their first birthday. Many older children also will die.

Children's deaths from disease, however, are fewer now than in the past. Thanks to organizations like UNICEF (United Nations Children's Fund), WHO (World Health Organization) and others, more and more children have been immunized or have been given oral rehydration therapy when suffering from diarrheal disease. However, greater numbers of children, in Bosnia, in Rwanda and elsewhere, have been killed or disabled or orphaned by wars and tribal conflicts, or have become refugees.

What is fully as tragic as the deaths, diseases and hunger of these children is abandonment by parents who have more children than they can support. Much of this child abandonment has occurred in the large LDC cities. There the abandoned children live in very dangerous conditions, amid filth from lack of sanitation, exploited and even maimed or killed by police.

31

Even if they live with their families, millions of LDC city children live in the poverty and squalor of shanty towns. With the growth of cities, LDC city governments are overwhelmed in their attempts to provide sewage and clean water for slum areas, as well as needed health services and schools.

But life for LDC rural children is also dangerous, for even though disease spreads less rapidly than in the cities, health care, when needed, is scarcer and farther away.

UNICEF has written that if the developed nations of the world would contribute $25 billion a year for ten years on behalf of the children of the LDCs, many problems could be solved. UNICEF claims that this amount would make it possible to eradicate most childhood diseases, provide needed nutrition for pregnant and nursing women, provide safe drinking water and obliterate illiteracy. UNICEF also has pointed out that wealthy countries such as the United States pay out more money than this for nonessentials. Americans spend $20 billion a year just on beer. Our annual so-called defense expenditure alone is many times that amount.

But it also should be noted that the LDCs themselves spend a total of over $125 billion a year on their military, in many cases spending an even greater proportion of their GNP than the United States spends.

Though I hope that our country and others will give the sort of aid that UNICEF describes, and which we certainly can afford, I am sure that much of the aid would fall through the cracks, due in part to the corruption and mishandling by native governments. I have witnessed much of this myself in the LDCs where I worked. We have already seen how great quantities of food sent to Somalia and other African countries have never reached the people most in need. In my own work in Africa and South Asia, I have seen how much of the money and supplies and equipment sent to benefit people and projects, were mishandled by the national governments.

Moreover, some of the health and other problems of LDCs cannot be solved without the exercise of authoritarian discipline. The Chinese accomplishments in health and development would not have taken place without the dictatorial measures by Mao and other leaders, coupled with the people's habits of submission to authority. Without such measures, age-old Chinese diseases would probably still be in place.

Despite all this, I suppose — and I hope — that UNICEF's objectives can ultimately be fulfilled. But this will require more than just money. It will take the sort of authority that will come hard. But if it saves the children, it will be worth it.

Children in the United States

Compared to the plight of children in the LDCs, the lot of most American children is indeed favorable. What Americans call poverty would be considered affluence by most LDC people. But millions of American children are subject to hazards that were almost unheard of only a few decades ago, crimes of violence, the drug traffic, sexual abuse and the breakdown of the family. Only 51 percent of all children under age 18 — 56 percent of white and only 26 percent of black — live in nuclear families with both of their own parents. The remainder live either in families headed by one parent, usually the mother, or with stepparents, grandparents or others. I will describe in a later chapter the sexual obsession in present-day American society, and much of the sexual abuse of children is committed by members of their own households, such as stepfathers or mothers' boyfriends.

American children also lack essential financial safeguards that would cost relatively little. I recommend that you read the 1991 report, entitled "Beyond Rhetoric", of the National Commission on Children. The report was the result of a very thorough study of the issues of health, education, social support, family support and the financial security of children. It described in great detail the hazards faced by children who lack adequate health care, particularly preventive care. The Commission studied the hazards faced by children in single-parent families, the environmental hazards faced by children growing up in substandard housing and in crime-ridden communities, the insecurity of children born into poverty and the tragedy of poor education.

While the Commission supported public family planning services and deplored teenage pregnancy, I felt that it could have said much more than it did about unwed and irresponsible childbearing in general. It should have pointed out that the decision to have a child requires more prayer, preparation and responsibility than any event in human life. While the Commission told of the disadvantages suffered by children whose parents separate or divorce, it said nothing about the extent to which separation and divorce flow from the sexual obsession in American society.

The Commission did make some noteworthy recommendations regarding the financial security of U.S. children and their families. It made new proposals to strengthen child support under the Family Support Act. One of the proposals calls for the Federal government to provide an insured child support benefit when absent parents do not pay or when the amount paid falls below an established minimum. The Commission also made proposals for welfare reform somewhat similar to the proposals made recently by President Clinton.

The Commission's most significant recommendation was that of an annual and refundable* child tax credit for all children under age 18. The initial amount of the tax credit recommended by the Commission was $1,000 per child, to be indexed annually to adjust for inflation. Its cost would be partially offset by elimination of the present child tax exemption. Its provision would also greatly reduce the need for welfare payments.

I will comment on this financial security recommendation, and make an alternative recommendation in my final chapter.

Family size

The Commission, other than commenting that some parents are unable to support their children, said nothing about family size. Its recommendation of a refundable tax credit for every child would apparently offer the same credit for a ninth child as for the first. My alternative recommendation will differ in this regard. But here I want to make some general comments on family size.

---

*By "refundable" is meant that any excess of the credit over income tax would be paid in cash as a sort of negative income tax. The earned income credit, already part of our tax system, operates in the same manner.

The World's Children

How disadvantaged, or how advantaged, are children in large families as compared with children with only one or two siblings, or an only child?

For years, it was said that an only child was a spoiled child. That his parents doted too much on him. That he grew up selfish because he was used to having everything he wanted. Children brought up in large families were usually considered to be of far better character because they had learned to share and cooperate with several siblings. The fact that they might individually have smaller shares of the family's goods didn't make them poorer; it taught them how to get along with less, and it therefore made them better citizens.

Large families were the rule in the United States prior to this century, and small families the exception. This was true in Europe as well. American presidents up through William McKinley had an average of four children, John Tyler had 15 (from two marriages), though James Polk had no children, George Washington had no children of his own, and James Buchanan never married. Families in Europe were also large, becoming smaller after 1850. Johann Sebastian Bach sired 20 children (from two marriages). Most of his children died in childhood, but three sons became famous composers.

Large families often had more difficulty in providing for individual children than smaller families, particularly in cities. Even though clothing could often be passed down from older children to younger, it was harder to divide food among several children. Children themselves recognized the hardships of having to share limited supplies with their siblings, and also sensed the economic burdens of their parents. Thomas Hardy's novel, "Jude the Obscure", told how a boy was so concerned over his family's economic situation, and over the fact that still another child was on the way, that he hanged his younger siblings and himself, and wrote the following message:

"Done because we are too menny"

Life today appears to be very difficult for a child if he or she is raised in a large family. Maybe it's because it is primarily the poor who have large families, but it seems that poor children in small families don't get into the troubles that face poor children in large families.

World Population Growth

The New York Times ran a series in May 1994 about killings in New York City committed by teenagers. Of the 26 cases reported, 21 involved children raised by single parents or by other relatives. No statistics on family size were presented, but wherever reference was made to other children in the teenager's household, their number was generally large, for example:

"Mrs. H___ and her eight children"

"T___ was living with his aunt and her seven children."

"P___ was the oldest of six children."

"R___ lived with his mother, ___, and several siblings.

G___ also lived with his mother, ___, and nine other siblings"

"C___ receives public assistance to raise J___ and seven other children."

Children's rights

In 1979 we had the International Year of the Child and in 1990 the World Summit on Children. Both were earnest in their attempt to bring much needed aid and hope to unfortunate children the world over.

In 1959 the UN issued the Declaration of the Rights of the Child, which enumerated ten fundamental rights. These included the following rights: adequate nutrition and health care, security, education, freedom from racial or religious discrimination, a home, a name and a nationality, freedom from exploitation, and special rights for handicapped children. Much has been written about these rights. Much has been said in the hope that they will be fully implemented.

The right to education implies another right that is not specifically enumerated in the Declaration, namely, the right to a job in which to use that education. One might call this the right to opportunity, the right to usefulness.

The World's Children

But there is another very important right that I would add, *the right not to be born.* Not to be born, that is, unless and until it can be assured that all of these other fundamental rights have a very good likelihood of fulfillment. That the child will not be born into deep poverty, handicap or a dangerous environment. The right not to be born means the right not to be born merely as a consequence of a sexual act or as a way of punishing child and parents for the parents' having had sex.

The right not to be born merely because of the parents' perceived economic, emotional or prestige needs. The right not to be born to supply a nation or a race or a tribe with more members, or with more fighters, or with more voters, or with more workers to exploit. The right not to be born because some members of a community believe that women should be compelled to become pregnant or be forced against their will to undergo childbirth. The right not to be born as an unwanted child. The right not to be born when a nation already has too many children to support. Or when a woman already has too many children. Or when her health or her age or the age of her last-born child indicate that she should not have a child now.

Think of all the misery in the world that might be avoided if this right not to be born were recognized.

Chapter 5

Women's Issues

"Women ...have large families because
that is expected of them."
— Nafis Sadik, executive director of
  the United Nations Population Fund

The roles taken by women and the attention paid to women's issues were the features of the Cairo Conference which distinguished it most from the earlier population conferences. At the 1974 and 1984 population conferences, women were present but were hardly heard. This time, a woman, Nafis Sadik of the UN Population Fund, organized the Conference, and she and other women had a substantial share in the drafting of the "Final Document" of the Conference. Women headed several of the national delegations to the Conference, though the U.S. delegation was led by Vice President Al Gore and the State Department's Deputy Secretary Tim Wirth.

One chapter of the Final Document is entitled "Gender Equality, Equity and Empowerment of Women." The title of this chapter speaks for itself, indicating that women want full equality with men in rights both in home and family and in the world of employment and the political process. The chapter calls for the elimination of all forms of discrimination against women, exploitation, harassment, violence and abuse. It also calls for male responsibility equal to women's in child-rearing and housework.

A later chapter is entitled "Reproductive Rights, Reproductive Health and Family Planning." Reproductive rights include the right of couples and individuals to decide "freely and responsibly" on the number of their children, and freedom from such coercion as forced abortion or forced sterilization. It was the wording in this chapter relating to means of controlling fertility that caused the greatest controversy during the Conference, since the Vatican and other delegations read into it the promotion of abortion, to which I will refer later.

Still another chapter deals largely with education of women as a fundamental requirement of development.

The position of women

Throughout human history, the situation of women has been one of subjection to men in one degree or another. In some societies even today, a woman is a chattel, not much different from an item of livestock, and in fact even acquired in exchange for livestock. Rather than being a companion to a husband, her value to him may lie only in serving his sexual needs, bearing his children, and performing the most drudging labor, both in the home and in agriculture. In Africa, in addition to all their work in the home and in child care, women bear the bulk of the work in raising food and also in marketing it. In LDCs where agriculture is partly mechanized, men operate the machines while women do the stoop labor and other arduous tasks.

Muslim writers defend the treatment of women under Islamic law as necessary for women's protection, but to Americans and European observers, Islam means the subjugation of women. In India and Sri Lanka, I found marked differences in status between Muslim and non-Muslim women. In both countries, even though only a small proportion of Hindu or Buddhist women took part in activities that brought them into the public eye, Muslim women were almost never in such activities. (Christian and Parsi women were the most active.) But even more obvious was the fact that Muslim women had the largest families.

In some Muslim countries, the actual situation of women is very pathetic. A man who can afford more than one wife may own as many as four, and cast off any wife at will and replace her by another, and keep the castoff wife's children if he wants them.

However, there is considerable variation in women's status as between one Islamic country and another. During Bourguiba's rule (1957-87), Tunisia underwent great modernization. Polygyny (having multiple wives) was prohibited, and women gained ready access to contraception and abortion (on demand). Tunisia now has the lowest TFR in the Arab world, and also the lowest infant and maternal mortality. Indonesia is another Islamic country where Muslim women enjoy considerable liberation.

Nevertheless, Islamic fundamentalism is threatening women's gains. Fundamentalists have tried to take over the government in Algeria, and if successful they may be a threat not only to women's rights but to the politics of all of North Africa. Fundamentalists even threatened the Conference itself by protest demonstrations in Egypt and elsewhere. Saudi Arabia and some other Islamic states boycotted the Conference.

Education of women has been a major development in most LDCs, and yet women's illiteracy persists. In India, for example, even though the percentages of female literacy have improved from one census to another, the actual number of illiterate women has actually been increasing. India's population increased by 24 percent between 1981 and 1991, and the total number of women in the population increased faster than the number of literate women.

Early childbearing also usually prevents a young woman from getting the education she needs to be economically independent. Also, education of itself has been found to be the most important factor leading to fertility reduction. The greater the number of years of schooling, the greater a woman's awareness of her own potentials and of economic opportunities, the greater her empowerment in her own family and in the community, the greater her likelihood of using a modern contraceptive method.

Women's reproductive health

The reproductive health issues which the Cairo Final Document addresses include health education, complications of pregnancy, prevention of maternal mortality, prevention of AIDS and other sexually transmitted diseases, availability of reproductive health information and care.

Quite aside from reproductive health, women are receiving poorer health care than men. In advanced countries such as our own, women's groups are protesting this, but in many LDCs there is not even opportunity to protest. Despite poorer health care and poorer nutrition, and despite maternal mortality, women now live longer than men in all MDCs and in most LDCs, but there are some exceptions. India is one country in which women's life expectancy at birth is less than men's by about a year, and its total female population is only about 93 percent of the total male.

Another issue was that of harmful cultural practices, such as genital mutilation, which often is inflicted on a girl in accordance with the wishes of family or community. Other issues were early marriage, arranged marriage, compelled marriage, dowry, or bride price, which also affect a woman's physical or mental health or dignity. In some societies girls are married and their marriages consummated before their first menstruation.

The main issue is still that of safe and effective family planning and its availability and acceptability. The objectives stated are help to enable couples to meet their reproductive goals — "to choose the number, spacing and timing of birth of their children", and "to prevent unwanted pregnancies and reduce the incidence of high-risk pregnancies and morbidity and mortality."

As indicated above, family planning methods must be safe as well as effective. Every female contraceptive method involves some health hazard or risk of discomfort. While the majority of contraceptive pill users have been free from complications, there is a sizable number of women who are not free. The same is true of every other female method. Women are safest when men use condoms or have had vasectomies, but in many cultures men refuse to assume contraceptive responsibility.

The abortion issue

Rather than supporting abortion, the Cairo Document repeats a statement of the 1984 Conference to the effect that abortion should not be promoted as a method of family planning, and that one of the purposes of family planning is to help women avoid abortion. Nevertheless, the Vatican and other representatives at the Conference pressed for the complete outlawing of abortion.

The real abortion issue is whether a
woman may be compelled to bear a child
child against her will.

On the opposite side, the woman Prime Minister of Norway called for the worldwide legality of abortion on demand. The abortion issue provided the most heated arguments at the Conference. But it is likely that the arguments gave more outside publicity to the Conference than it would otherwise have had and therefore increased world attention to population matters.

A related issue was that of the prevention of adolescent pregnancy. The wording in the Document appeared to Vatican and other delegates to encourage sexual permissiveness among teenage women, including such words and expressions as "self-determination", "rights to privacy" and "access of adolescents to the services ... they need." This wording implied adolescents' rights to both contraception and legal abortion.

In actual fact, however, abortion will still be a decision great numbers of women will opt for, whether it is illegal or not. Where abortion is legal, it is usually safe. But illegal abortion involves the risk of serious health complications. Worldwide, there may be as many as 20 million illegal abortions annually.

A study has been made in six Latin American countries where abortion is illegal, Brazil, Chile, Colombia, the Dominican Republic, Mexico, and Peru. An estimated 2.8 million abortions take place annually in these countries. The estimated annual number of hospitalizations for abortion complications is 550,000. In Chile, 35 percent of all pregnancies result in abortion. That means that there is at least one abortion for every two live births.

The real question in regard to abortion is: *Is it right to compel a women to bear a child against her will?*

Also, the only way to prevent abortions is to prevent unwanted pregnancies. The politically powerful "pro-life" organizations in the United States that either oppose contraception or that take no position on it or believe that legal prohibition will stop abortions are not realistic. Millions of the abortions that have been performed in Latin America, as well as abortion-related deaths, have resulted from Catholic-ordered denial of rights to contraception.

Protection and empowerment of girls and women

Female infanticide, which was common in India and some other countries earlier in this century, is now fairly rare. However, girl children are often unwelcome and often receive much poorer nutrition and care than boys. A major concern in Hindu families is the large dowry that must be paid to secure husbands for their daughters. Now that amniocentesis and ultrasound are available in Indian cities, clinics advertise these procedures, pointing out that it is far cheaper to have a sex-determination test and abort a female fetus now, than to have to pay a dowry years later.

The dowry itself has also come under attack, though it is unlikely that much can be done about it. Dowries have been illegal in India for many years, and yet in some areas and among some castes they are almost universal. Another practice is that of persecuting, and even murdering, young brides when a groom's family becomes dissatisfied with the amount of dowry.

It is largely due to women's insistence on smaller families that fertility rates have dropped dramatically in countries like Colombia, Mexico, Panama, Indonesia, Thailand, Tunisia and South Korea. But there are a number of countries where most women still want anywhere from four to six surviving children, so that the mere availability of contraception will not hold back population growth. Even women who would be content with two or fewer children are likely to find their partners wanting more children.

Women writers complain that family-planning programs are too often run by men, even when most of the direct outreach to women is by women paramedics. They complain that the programs are too contraceptive-driven, meaning that their success is measured too much in terms of numbers of family-planning acceptors and numbers of births averted (i.e., the extent to which programs and program methods reduce the number of births). The result, they claim, is that women are regimented instead of being treated humanely. This complaint is valid, as I know from my own work in South Asia, where I was involved in such cost-effectiveness studies. There are some claims that the fertility reductions which have taken place in South Asia would have taken place anyhow had there been no efforts other than a combination of population education with economic development. For reasons which are too complex to explain here, I personally question such claims. I feel that there is a real need for *both* economic development and family-planning programs.

On the other hand, it is certainly true that women deserve and need great economic support. Once women have opportunities for earning substantial income, they will both have more power to make and enforce their own fertility decisions and also feel less need for children on whom to rely for financial security either now or in old age.

As it is particularly desirable to discourage early childbearing, efforts should be made to prevent pressuring young women into early marriages, many of which are unstable or involve oppression by the husband or his family. This is why it is so necessary that there be economic opportunities for young women.

In societies where many women are sexually active before marriage, it is important to provide services to prevent pregnancies that would either force a woman into marriage or bring economic disaster to her and her child. Early pregnancy lengthens the number of years over which a woman will bear children, and therefore keeps fertility higher.

Male roles and responsibilities

Men should be led to exercise a greater role in fertility reduction, both through a more active sharing of birth control responsibility and an increased activity in child rearing. Even when men accept the need for birth control, the responsibility for it is generally thrown on women. It is women who use the Pill and IUDs, even though these can adversely affect their health or comfort. Women use these methods, as well as diaphragms, because men refuse to use condoms, which they can do with ease. Because women realize the cost of frequent childbearing to themselves and their children, it is usually they, rather than men, who undergo sterilization operations. The female operation usually requires hospitalization and recovery time. When a man gets a vasectomy, it is a five-minute outpatient procedure.

In too many societies, even in developed countries, men have had so little responsibility in the care and rearing of children that they fail to realize how high the child's cost is and how great the burden of motherhood. In societies with high fertility, it is often found that fathers have little part in the daily life of their children, except for association with older sons. Wherever fertility is as low as replacement level or lower, it is often because men have taken an active share in their children's care as well as in their financial support.

Women's rights and responsibilities

Even those women's advocates who emphasize women's rights to limit the number of childbirths, also insist on a woman's right to bear as many children as she wants. Declarations of this and previous conferences give women and couples the right to choose "freely and responsibly" the number of their children. But just what is responsible? Isn't there a possible conflict between "freely" and "responsibly"? Do the advocates who claim for women the right to have as many children as they want concede that exercising this right may injure the rights of the community or of other persons?

A woman should give consideration to her family's and her community's or society's welfare, and how this welfare may be affected by her decision to bear a large number of children. But every child should have the right not to be born unless and until all the child's other fundamental rights are in place, a right which I declared in the preceding chapter. Is it fair to a child for a woman to bear her or him if she knows, or should know, that the child will suffer economic or social disadvantage, or impaired health, or be unwanted? Is it loving to the child or to others to bear her or him under such conditions?

Heroic women

Few of us men have real appreciation for the heroism of women, not only as wives and mothers, but as performers of the most arduous tasks in the economy, whether that of developing countries or our own.

And how many of us know the heroism women are exhibiting today in their efforts for fundamental reform in nations and the world? How many know about Nobel peace prize winner Aung San Suu Kyi? She is the woman who for years led the fight for democracy in Myanmar (formerly known as Burma), on behalf of men as well as of women. She was kept under house arrest for at least five years. Though she has now been released, her future status is uncertain.

Women's Issues

I have already referred to Islamic fundamentalism as a growing threat to the rights of women. It can best be described as a movement designed to "keep women in their place." Surprisingly, however, some predominantly Muslim countries have women as prime ministers, despite strong fundamentalist opposition. Khaleda Zia, the widow of an assassinated former prime minister, is now prime minister of Bangladesh, and Hasina Wazed, daughter of another assassinated former prime minister, heads the main opposition party. Still another Bangladesh woman, Taslina Nasrin, was forced into hiding when fundamentalists pronounced a death sentence on her for her writings critical of Islam's treatment of women. Her case is parallel to that of Salman Rushdie, who is under death threat by Iran fundamentalists because of his writings.

Still another woman, Benazir Bhutto, is prime minister for the second time in Pakistan, where fundamentalism is even stronger than in Bangladesh. Her father, a former prime minister, had been ousted from power and then put to death by his successor. At the Cairo Conference, Prime Minister Bhutto, even though opposed to abortion, helped to work out a compromise position on that issue.

As brutal toward women as Islamic fundamentalism seems to be, my many male Muslim friends show no trace of brutality. On the contrary, they are as gentle and devoted to their wives and as respectful of their wives' rights as men anywhere.

Abortion

The final document of the Cairo Conference contains a statement on abortion which begins as follows: "In no case should abortion be promoted as a method of family planning." It goes on to highlight the public health concern over unsafe abortions and to give the highest priority to the prevention of unwanted pregnancies, stating that "all attempts should be made to eliminate the need for abortion." The statement recognizes that individual governments may continue to treat abortion as illegal, but states that abortion should be safe wherever it is legal.

One would think that there could be little objection to this statement. Yet, no American pro-life organization is willing to admit that there can ever be a "need" for abortion, except where the woman's life is clearly at risk.

Moreover, even though it should be obvious that there could be no abortions if there were no unwanted pregnancies, these same organizations deny any need for contraception. The American Life League and Catholics United for Life would argue that all birth control (except perhaps the rhythm method) is almost as evil as abortion and that its use leads to the acceptance of abortion.

Other organizations, such as the National Right-to-Life Committee and Americans United for Life would say that while they do not oppose contraception, it is not part of their agenda. That strict legal prohibition -- not contraception -- is the only effective way to prevent abortion.

But I will admit that the pro-life people have one strong point on their side, namely that easy abortion has invited sexual irresponsibility. At a meeting some years ago sponsored by "pro-choice" groups, I heard a speaker express gratitude that the Roe vs. Wade decision had taken all the worry out of sex.

The audience applauded her, but I asked myself whether there shouldn't be some worry in sex. Whether there should or not, AIDS has put back into sex some of the worry that Roe vs. Wade took away.

Chapter 6

Food or Famine

"World resources of agricultural land can feed, at [American]
standards, 47 billion people ... For people living at
[Asian] standards ... 157 billion people."
— Colin Clark

With world population growing the way it is, will there be food enough for tomorrow's children? Or will millions of them die of hunger?

Opinions vary. In the late 1960s, there were dire predictions. The title of the Paddock brothers' book, "Famine, 1975", was enough to frighten large numbers of people who never even read the book. On the other side, the British economist Colin Clark has written that the world can feed 47 billion people (eight times the present world population), even if all enjoyed an American diet. If the world's people could content themselves with an Asian diet, Clark says, more than three times that number can be fed.

People find in their research what they want to find. Dr. Clark documented his findings with a great amount of investigation and calculation, all of which appear in his books. But Clark was also a lay member of Pope Paul VI's commission to review Church teachings on birth control, and was one of the few members to support those teachings. One wonders whether he was trying to fortify his own religious beliefs with his agricultural findings, or vice versa.

Except for people who like Clark would welcome great increases in population, it is dubious that many today would believe that a world population of 47 billion humans can be fed with

49

any livable diet. My own belief, however, is that with proper management the earth can produce enough food for at least twice its present population. But this would require much belt-tightening by those who are now well-fed. And it would also raise American food prices to a much larger share of our living costs.

Until recently, agricultural capacity in the United States seemed limitless. No more. Although we have been blessed with a very abundant and inexpensive water supply, that supply is now dwindling. California is one of the world's greatest food suppliers, furnishing vegetables and fruits to many millions of Americans, as well as rice to people in developing countries. But one of California's most troubling crises today is its water shortage, resulting in part from California's rapid population growth.

Topsoil depletion is also threatening the world's long-range agricultural production. Deforestation the world over, along with deep-plowing practices in the effort to get more food, combine to raise questions about how much longer food can be produced as cheaply and abundantly as it can today.

The world's food situation is therefore a serious long-range problem, but certainly not the world's most immediate one. People are starving in Africa and malnourished in many parts of the world, but food is available to feed them. When the world chooses to send emergency food to Africa, the food is available. Other problems related to population growth, such as civil and political tensions and conflicts, the movements of large numbers of desperate people, the crowding of people in urban areas, the accumulation of undisposed waste, the shortages of potable water, are far more immediate threats than mass starvation.

Even though Clark's statements are exaggerated, they are useful in illustrating how excessive the American diet is in relation to nutritional needs. That excess is marked most in the consumption of meat. The following table shows per capita consumption of meat (beef, pork, mutton, lamb and poultry) of the U.S. and several other countries during 1990, based on carcass weight in kilograms:

Food or Famine

United States	112	Soviet Union	70
Australia	104	Brazil	47
France	91	Japan	41
Germany	89	Mexico	40
Argentina	82	China	24
Italy	77	Egypt	14
U.K.	71	India	2

Perhaps we should have stopped when we got to China, as it is well known that large proportions of the Egyptian and Indian populations are malnourished. Though India has plenty of cattle, Indians use them mostly for milk and as draft animals.

An American family that owns a dog or cat may feed its pet more meat in the form of pet food than the meat eaten by an entire human family in many LDCs.

An additional, and very important, factor is that the beef Americans consume comes from grain-fed cattle, whereas cattle in other parts of the world are mostly grazed. Our poultry and pork are also grain-fed. We therefore not only consume more meat than anyone else, but our meat is produced at much higher cost. Animals account for 70 percent of our grain consumption.

Counting the grain fed to our animals, it therefore takes much more grain to feed Americans than to feed anyone else. The students at the population study center in Ghana where I taught during 1980 and 1982 used to tell me that each American eats 15 times as much food as what goes into an African mouth. I knew that this was an exaggeration, but it took a little while for me to get to the bottom of their story. What happened was this: Somebody had stated that it takes 15 times as much grain to produce a unit of protein from the meat of grain-fed animals as from grain eaten directly. When this reasonably correct report reached the African newspapers, it was distorted into the account the students gave me. Fair enough!

Whether livestock are grazed or grain fed, they have a major environmental cost in the amount of former forest land that had to be devoted either to the pastures where livestock graze or to planting the crops which they consume. But grain feeding is by far the more expensive so far as land use is concerned, since cropland is scarcer and more valuable. Also, great amounts of fossil fuel are required in grain production, both in manufacturing fertilizers and in fueling farm machinery.

There are several other costs to be considered in meat production: water for livestock, pollution from fertilizer and manure runoff, and overgrazing that converts grassland into deserts.

The message is clear: In the face of growing world population, it is essential that humans, and particularly we Americans, learn to rely less on consumption of meat.

What proved the Paddock brothers wrong in predicting widespread famine and starvation in the 1970s was the "green revolution" of that decade, the technological changes that increased food production not only in advanced countries but also in developing countries. India, which had to import great quantities of food in the 1960s to keep its people alive, became a net food exporter in the 1980s. Some of the agricultural potential that Colin Clark described has seemed to come about. But, even ignoring the environmental cost, the increase in productivity cannot go on forever.

According to the Worldwatch Institute, the annual rate of increase in world food production has slipped from 3 percent, which once was greater than the annual increase in world population, to about 1 percent, which is now less than the current 1.6 percent rate of population growth.

What's more, even though a world food crisis now seems less imminent, millions of people are underfed or malnourished. Indian peasants, though not starving, are not too far from starvation. Millions of Africans actually are starving. Much of their present starvation results from wartime conditions that prevent proper production and distribution of food. But even without this there would be a marked food deficiency. With its high rate of population increase, Africa will be increasingly dependent on food from outside the continent.

But, as already noted, a shortage of food is not the worst or the most immediate crisis stemming from population growth. Political and civil tensions and conflicts are the most immediate threat.

Chapter 7

Environment

"Ye shall not pollute the land wherein ye are."
— The Book of Numbers (35:33)

What sort of a physical environment are we leaving for our children, and for their children and their children's children? Or we might even ask, what sort of an environment have we left for ourselves?

At the beginning of this century, far more of the United States was covered with forest than today. Lakes and rivers were clean and full of fish, even without being stocked. Air was so pure that even city people could look up at night and see the wonder of the Milky Way. How many of today's children even know that there is a Milky Way unless they live far from a city? How many different animals, birds, and plants are there that children saw then, which today's children may never see?

Our own population growth and the increased concentration of population in metropolitan areas have been an important cause of environmental deterioration. But our failure to regulate land use has played an even larger role. Forests and wetlands have been sacrificed to farm expansion and suburban development.

But the depletion of forests, of marine life, of pure air, of biologic species is not limited to the United States. It is worldwide. The great tropical rain forests, and great highland forests, are cut down to make room for agricultural and grazing land. Here too, the biologic species these forests sheltered are endan-

53

gered or extinct. Marine life in the world's oceans, though not harvested to the point of extinction, is seriously depleted.

Industrial pollution of water and air is even greater in some less developed countries than here. In Bombay, India, industrial fumes are almost suffocating, and the entire city reeks of stale urine. The combination of population density and poverty is deadly. The city is too poor to provide public toilets for the thousands who live on the streets; it is also too poor to afford the pollution control technologies used in the United States.

The same combination of population and poverty is at work in agricultural societies too. We blame the peasants in the exploding population of Nepal for cutting down more trees for fuel than can be replanted. But we overlook the fact that they do not have the access to the energy sources we have, and thus must destroy the forests. Because of population growth, subsistence farmers have to plant and graze and exhaust more and more land. They cannot afford soil conservation measures, such as letting part of their land lie fallow.

In the LDCs, where population pressure has led to deforestation, overgrazing and overcropping, land has become so blighted that millions of people have become "environmental refugees", and people must leave in order to survive. In Africa, people are forced to leave home by combined famine and wars. Wars are fought over resources that would have been adequate for the smaller populations of the past but are greatly inadequate now.

Our own behavior

The United States has been called "the most overpopulated nation", meaning that we consume and pollute more than other nations, not merely per capita but also in relation to our geographic area. With respect to gasoline consumption, this is almost certainly the case. There are many environmental issues involving our own behavior I could discuss in this chapter, but the one I'll highlight is the consumption of gasoline.

How do you go to work each day? By train, by bus, on foot, in a friend's car or in your own? If you drive, how difficult is it for you to park when you get to work, and how much does it cost?

54

Environment

According to data compiled by the 1990 U.S. census, 86 percent of us go to work by private car, truck or van, and seven out of eight of these drive alone. If you doubt the latter statistic, just stand along the highway and count cars and passengers.

I realize that some of the cars that people drive are not parked in one spot all day but are needed when their drivers go from one customer or workplace to another. But polls show that most are used simply for the round trip to and from work, at a substantial weekly cost just to cover gas and parking. Many drivers I know tell me they don't know why they drive. They realize that driving doesn't necessarily save time, since many buses use special lanes which enable them to speed past traffic jams in the regular lanes. They also realize that they can't read or write or do other work while driving, though as a bus or train passenger they could. Many of them admit that the only excuse they have for driving is that they like the privacy of their own cars.

But what an environmental cost to pay for privacy! Car drivers deplete petroleum reserves, pollute the air, necessitate the use of more precious space for roads and parking places, and slow down public buses which could otherwise transport everybody much faster.

This is just one of the ways in which we of the United States are hurting the environment. Some of the other MDCs do much the same as we, but in energy consumption we are the worst. Our per capita consumption of energy is three times as great as highly industrialized Japan's, six times as great as Mexico's, 33 times as great as India's.

In addition to this, we of the United States throw away durable items after using them only a few times, and in the process we waste valuable materials and saturate our landfills. We can commit all this environmental damage because we're rich. The poor of the world can't even afford the things we throw away, but if they could, they would take better care of them and make better use of them.

Even the destruction of LDC forests is partly our fault. Our desire for cheap beef has prompted Latin Americans to cut down valuable forests to graze cattle to supply us with hamburgers. Marine life in tropical waters is harvested to satisfy American desire for proteins, proteins which the poor need more than we, but can't afford.

World Population Growth

Yes, population growth does play a major role in despoiling the environment. And just as we can't blame everything on population, the poor nations can't blame everything on poverty. The fact that people are poor doesn't fully excuse them from having too many children. But often the women who have many children did not have them out of choice; they may have had them to maintain status or to satisfy their husbands. Or they lacked the information and the means to have fewer.

I have touched on only a few of the many aspects of the world's environmental crisis. But the fact remains, that the adult population of today, whether in LDCs or MDCs, are leaving a poorer environment for our children than what our parents left for us.

Chapter 8

The Effects of Overcrowding

"The land was not able to bear them that
they might dwell together"
— The Book of Genesis (13:6)

To what extent does overcrowding cause anti-social attitudes and actions?

The near future will witness the development of new energy sources -- sun, wind, tides, etc. -- and more abundant water from the desalinization of ocean water. While these may lessen our concerns over physical resources, the problems of human crowding and interaction will worsen as population increases.

Overcrowding has been felt by mankind for centuries. The book of Genesis tells how Abraham and Lot tried living together with their many herdsmen. But the crowding was so great that there was strife among the herdsmen, and the only solution was for the two households to go their separate ways.

In the Introduction, I implied that the 1994 tragedy in Rwanda was a population-related disaster.

At the very least, the number of casualties would have been much lower had the population been much smaller. But I am also convinced that high population density contributed significantly to the savage tribal warfare which has taken place, not only in Rwanda, but also in recent years in neighboring Burundi. Both countries have similar population densities, rapid population growth, and the same warring tribes, the usually dominant Tutsis and the more numerous but less powerful Hutus. In the previous chapter, I described how African wars have been fought over resources that are too scarce for today's increased populations, and this was certainly a factor in the wars in Rwanda and Burundi.

I cannot prove much more than that, as applied to these particular countries. But scholars such as Nazli Choucri have written persuasively about the population factor operating in many earlier conflicts. Choucri has described almost a hundred conflicts during the period 1945-1969 alone which she considers population-related. None of these local "wars" were formally declared, but they did involve serious casualties.

Two of her wars involved countries to which I will refer later. One was the Dominican Republic's conflict with Haiti in 1963; another Honduras's conflict with El Salvador in 1969, the so-called "soccer war." In each case, conflict resulted from the overflow of people from an overcrowded country, Haiti or El Salvador, into a less crowded Dominican Republic or Honduras, provoking resentment by the people of the less crowded country. All four countries had and still have natural increase rates exceeding 2 percent, and all four have tripled in population since 1950, counting the large numbers of Salvadorans and Haitians who have emigrated.

There is considerable literature on the effect of overcrowding on the behavior of animals. The laboratory experiments on animals show that overcrowding produces highly anti-social and even violent conduct. Animals in an overcrowded environment will fight with each other even when there are sufficient food and resources for all. Humans apparently are not affected in the same way. When there is a shortage of essential resources, they search for methods to expand the resources.

But several observers have found that, even though high population density may be unlikely to affect human behavior, population growth can have considerable effect. In the Introduction, I contrasted Rwanda with Japan. The former has two tribes with a history of conflict and an increasing population caused by high fertility. Japan, though with a high density, has both a homogeneous population and very low population growth.

Haiti has a relatively homogeneous population, though photographs show that a few of the ruling class, especially Lt. General Cedras, have European skin color, hair and features rather than African. But my impression of the majority of the Haitian people is that they have overbred to such an extent that they have weakened themselves not only economically but also politically. In a later chapter, I will quote the views of Jacques-Yves Cousteau on the overbreeding by the Haitian poor.

High-density living

Loss of personal privacy is an effect of population crowding to which some writers attribute an adverse effect. Many persons need privacy to conceal from others their own personal weaknesses. Having to behave in one's own way without being closely observed by too many others gives individuals a greater feeling of security. Even a strong feeling of privacy within one's own family may be a personal need.

But in some cultures and some strata of society, the privacy need is only between families, not within a family. When my wife and I were housed in the USAID Staff House in Delhi, we had the use of a separate apartment in which to house our servants. That apartment consisted of only one main room, about nine-by-nine feet in dimension, plus a tiny cooking area and a tiny bathroom. The apartment had electricity, a ceiling-fan and running water.

Unlike many USAID families, we had only one servant, a Muslim man whose family lived far from Delhi. He was so delighted with the tiny apartment provided for him, that he asked if he could bring his family to Delhi to live there with him. When he told us that he had six children, we put our foot down. So he said he would leave two children behind with relatives and bring only his wife and the youngest four. We reluctantly consented, but he nevertheless brought all six, and we didn't have the heart to send the oldest two back. But just a few weeks later, a seventh child was born, and the family of nine continued to live in their nine-by-nine quarters in perfect harmony. When the oldest daughter married, the number of occupants was reduced to eight. But on a subsequent visit to see her family, she brought another young woman with her, bringing the number temporarily to 10. Even then, their huge household seemed to function harmoniously.

World Population Growth

High-density living of a different form has sometimes been proposed for the United States, both as an argument that we can absorb more immigration and also as a conservation measure. U.S. metropolitan areas are beset with what is called "urban sprawl", the spreading of population into suburbs, which are sometimes so far out that the rural nature of outlying land is wholly lost. An additional effect of urban sprawl is that it is impracticable to accommodate outlying population with public transportation, so that the automobile must be used for long-distance commuting. (We should note, however, the automobile is extensively used even where efficient public transportation facilities exist.)

If the entire metropolitan population could be housed in a concentrated area, mostly in high-rise apartment buildings, everyone would be near work or school or shopping, and there would be no real need for private cars. This would result in great energy saving and also eliminate the need for the large-scale parking facilities that now exist. (For the relatively few people who would need or own cars, the cars could be parked in designated storage areas at the city limits.)

Conservationists have often advocated high-density living like this, not only because of the greatly reduced use of cars, but also because rural areas would be left unspoiled instead of being "suburbanized."

New York City is sometimes named as a moderately successful example of high-density living. It has, of necessity, managed to get along without too many privately-owned motor vehicles. It has a fairly high crime rate, though most of its crime is outside of Manhattan, which is the most densely settled borough, with most residents living in high-rise apartments.

What about children in high-density living?

Our servant's children thrived, despite the sort of living which most Americans would liken to sardines in a sardine can. But their living in our servant's quarters, while perhaps more crowded than what they had been used to, was in other respects probably far better than before, partly because of our solicitude and provision for them. Before they came to us, two of the family's children had died.

In comparison, the situation of children in Rwandan or other high-density African countries must be miserable, even in relatively peaceful times. Other things being equal, transmission

The Effects of Overcrowding

of childhood disease is more rapid in crowded areas, with a probable high correlation between crowding and mortality.

In our own cities, many low-cost high-density housing projects have become notorious for drug abuse, gang violence and other crime. Whatever may be the advantages on the side of high-density living as opposed to urban sprawl, there's much to be said about the disadvantages in terms of human relations. If taking in great numbers of immigrants and refugees means that both they and we must live in increasingly crowded conditions, this can hardly be an argument supporting immigration.

Chapter 9

Births and Deaths of Children

*"It came to pass on the seventh day that
[King David's] child died"*
— The Second Book of Samuel (12:18)

Isn't the high death rate of children in the developing world responsible for the high birth rate? Isn't that the reason for birth rates in the LDCs not having declined faster than they have?

Before answering, let me point out that fertility has declined rather rapidly in some of the LDCs. You must remember that fertility in Europe declined slowly too, but its decline started much earlier and before mortality had declined very far. Fertility decline in the LDCs started late, but now that the decline has started it is just as fast in some countries as European fertility decline was.

Yes, child mortality is one of the factors for the continuation of high fertility, though as we shall see it is not an overriding factor. Another factor is the relation of the costs of having children to the perceived benefits of having them. Still another is the status of women, which we have already discussed.

Whenever fertility has declined in human history, the decline seldom took place unless child mortality decline preceded it. But there have been places where fertility didn't decline, or declined very little, even in the face of substantial decline in infant and child mortality. There are several possible reasons for this.

One is that having or not having children is not necessarily a matter of conscious decision. *People have children because they*

63

have sex, and although they may have strong preferences as to how many children they should have, these preferences do not always govern fertility outcome.

Another is that people don't recognize how much mortality has declined, and they therefore still believe that they must have a large number of children in order for a sufficient number to survive. I was involved in a study about 1970 in Punjab State in India. Infant and child mortality had declined substantially. Yet when the parents in 22 villages were surveyed, only 29 percent said that they believed child survival was better than in their own childhood, and almost an equal percentage — 26 percent — believed that it had worsened. The remaining 45 percent either had no opinion or believed there had been no change.

In 1930 the U.S. infant mortality rate was 60 (i.e., 60 deaths per 1,000 live births), and life expectancy at birth was 60 years. Yet our fertility was actually below replacement level, despite the fact that the only methods of contraception were the condom and diaphragm. Abortion was illegal. Today almost all Latin American and Caribbean countries have infant mortality below 60 and life expectancy above 60 (Haiti is the notable exception). Yet their fertility is in most cases well above replacement level (Cuba is an exception).

The point I want to make is that high fertility in most of today's developing countries cannot be rationalized on the basis of high infant or child mortality. Our country had low fertility in 1930 despite relatively high mortality because: (1) we were sufficiently educated to know the disadvantages of large families, (2) except for Roman Catholics, we were subject to relatively few traditional or cultural influences calling for large families, and (3) we were already more an industrialized than an agricultural society.

In the developing world, there are factors beside mortality that keep fertility high. Some factors are economic, but one that I should mention here is that it is not sufficient to have several children in many LDCs. There must also be surviving *sons,* and sometimes parents have many daughters before even one son is born. Daughters often do not count, since when they marry they will become part of another family, and in most traditional societies only sons are in a position to support aged parents.

Births and Deaths of Children

In my years in India, I found that even in the cities parents wanted two sons, in rural areas sometimes three sons. One daughter might suffice, but if parents keep on having children until a second son is born, they will on average have two daughters as well, an average of four children, unless they detect and abort a female fetus.

In terms of number of surviving children, families in most developing countries are larger now than ever before. Years ago, an LDC woman who lived to age 50 would typically have had seven children of whom only two or three survived to adulthood, while today her granddaughter, who has married later and who sometimes uses contraception, may typically have five children of whom at least four will survive.

In some countries where substantial reductions of infant and child mortality have taken place, there has so far been virtually no reduction in fertility. In Jordan and Syria, for example, infant mortality is now less than 50 per 1,000, also less than U.S. infant mortality of the early 1930s, and yet fertility is not much below its traditional level. People in Jordan and Syria and in several other countries still want large families, and the decrease in infant mortality has made it easier to have them.

There is no set relationship of mortality and fertility that will fit every country or every culture. In some parts of Europe, notably in France, fertility began to decline even while infant mortality was very high. One of the factors which affected fertility within Europe was the extent of celibacy and of late marriage.

Desirable though reduction of infant and child mortality is for its own sake, it is now more likely to accelerate population growth than to retard it

Even when reduction of infant and child mortality reduces fertility, it is unlikely that the mortality reduction will reduce the rate of population growth. Reduction of infant and child mortality has been the major factor causing population growth, and it is so powerful a factor that it will likely outweigh whatever fertility decline it causes.

65

World Population Growth

If mortality reduction reduces fertility, it is even more true that fertility reduction reduces infant and child mortality. It is now recognized that the probabilities of infant and child death are increased when children are born to very young mothers or to mothers who have already had many pregnancies or when successive births are too close together — too young, too many, too quickly. The effect of the mother being too young will be discussed in a later chapter. Births that are too closely spaced may impair the health of both the older of the two children and that of the younger, in one case because breast feeding is shortened, in the other because of the weakening of the mother. Children after the mother's second or third born have increasingly high infant mortality; eighth born children have been found to have infant mortality triple that of second born, and it has been estimated that if no mother were to have more than three children, infant mortality would on the average decrease by 8 percent.

One way parents in the developing world can help the survival of their children is not to have too many children in the first place. Having fewer additional children will help the survival of the children already here.

Chapter 10

Children's Values and Costs

*"If I didn't have my sons, I wouldn't have half
the prosperity I do"*
— Indian village potter quoted by Mahmood Mamdani

There is no doubt that in some LDCs, particularly in agricultural settings, children can have great economic value. When I was teaching at an international population study center in Ghana, a Ghanaian student invited me to his family's farm for the weekend. It was time to harvest the corn (maize) crop, and the men did the cutting and then lifted heavy baskets of corn onto the women's heads. After the women carried the baskets to the storage shed, I was there to take the baskets off their heads and stack the corn. But among the "women" was a five-year old girl who carried a basket almost as heavy as her mother's, and a three-year old boy was carrying a small basket in his arms. That went on all day, and had I thought to bring my camera along, the pictures of these children would be on these pages.

I said that children *may* have great economic value to their parents. But the picture is not a consistent one. In Sri Lanka I spent many days in villages, and noticed that while girls were kept busy at home after school adjourned (usually at 1:00 PM), boys loitered together "in town". In larger villages they attended the local movie. This is of course what most boys do if they can get away with it. Sri Lanka is a more modernized country than Ghana, and conditions which we associate with cities spread to the rural areas, much as they do in our own country.

World Population Growth

But even in cities girls have their economic values in the home, and some boys have economic value on the streets. They do errands for passersby and for tourists as well as for their own families, they solicit, they beg, they steal. They are ubiquitous; city streets are alive with children, especially boys.

Many books and articles have been published dealing with the value of children in developing societies. It has sometimes been claimed that children are so valuable that there can be little or no desire for birth control. A book by Mahmood Mamdani, entitled "The Myth of Population Control," reported his findings in the Indian Punjab about 1970. The men whom Mamdani interviewed indicated an urgent economic need for large families, particularly for several sons. Those who owned land were aware that having several sons would present the problem of fragmentation of their land holdings, but this concern was secondary to the need for the sons' — and even daughters' — labor. But even the landless were equally desirous of having several sons for the income the sons would bring them; they were sure the sons would be able to send remittances home after going to the cities for jobs.

Though it is true that people believe they must have sons for support in old age, the sons will often fail to provide support

People's ideas may be reasonable but be based on incorrect knowledge. U.S. Peace Corps volunteers in western India told me that they had also questioned farm smallholders in the area where they worked, and asked questions similar to those asked by Mamdani, and received somewhat similar answers. The area was one which had been a maharaja's hunting forest but was turned over to the peasants when the maharajas had to give up their lands in 1947. Some of the answers were, "My father and my brothers and I came here and cut down the trees to make farms, and my sons will go elsewhere in India and cut down the trees there." Others said their sons would get good jobs in Bombay. In both cases the answers seemed reasonable enough, but only because the men weren't aware of what had happened to both trees and jobs.

Children's Values and Costs

While I never attempted scientific surveys of my own, I too would ask acquaintances about their children's future economic prospects. I often got the impression that they had never given serious thought to the subject, being confident that their sons would take care of them just as they had taken care of their own parents.

More recent studies describing the economic dependence of older parents on their grown sons reveal the fact that sons are not providing their parents with the old-age support the parents had counted on. Adult sons and daughters are not finding jobs. I personally knew middle-aged people who were still supporting grown sons and daughters.

When LDC societies become more modernized and urbanized, and also as agriculture becomes more mechanized, the economic value of children to their parents lessens. Moreover, their economic cost increases, because the more modern the society the more must be spent on education and on clothing and other modern items. Because children live longer, and because health care has become modernized, more must be spent on their health. Children are still an economic asset, but in a different sense; the child's value is his value to himself even more than to his parents. The parents have already made considerable investment in that child's value (to himself) in giving him birth, in caring for him and in educating him, and they must put in more investment to protect the investment they have already made. The quality of life of each of the few children they will have becomes much more important than the quantity of children. Having a large number of children can become an intolerable expense, just as it could well be in our own society.

Also, a few modernizing societies have now developed institutional mechanisms, including social security systems and pension plans, and health care systems for the elderly, which lessen the need for older parents to depend economically on children. Also in some of these societies, parents no longer rely on their children for housing.

Chapter 11

Other Factors Affecting Fertility

"George, two children is just the right number for our family, one to replace Dad and one to replace me."
— My mother, explaining why she had only two children

Ever since the 1950s, surveys have been conducted in developing countries, in which women, and sometimes men also, have been asked their opinions about desired family size and what might be done to achieve it. Often the women who are surveyed are also asked what they know about birth control methods, what they think about them, and whether they use them.

In some LDCs, however, it was found that women could not express the number of children they desired. They were so fatalistic that they appeared never to have asked themselves the question. Many therefore replied, "Up to God", or gave some equally indefinite answer. Others gave answers which were influenced by their expected norm; in countries where there were large numbers of both Muslims and non-Muslims, Muslim women had the higher fertility and also indicated the higher preference.

On the other hand, we do find in many LDCs a breaking away from traditional and religious influence, just as we have seen in the case of American Catholics. Even the differential between Muslim and non-Muslim fertility is diminishing in Malaysia and Indonesia, where government-sponsored birth control programs have had a fair measure of success. In other countries with a large Muslim population, Muslim fertility is still higher than non-Muslim.

World Population Growth

In Latin America, as well as in the United States, Catholic teachings against birth control are losing their hold. As I shall mention in a later chapter, even Catholic priests are giving tacit consent to modern contraception, partly because they sympathize with the plight of women and partly because they realize that without the use of contraceptives, women may resort to abortion.

The advent of modern birth control methods

Modern birth control was rarely available in developing countries until "family planning" programs were sponsored by the West. Sponsors believed that contraceptives, once introduced, would be eagerly accepted by LDC people, but this seldom proved to be the case. People either felt that birth control was unnecessary and undesirable, or they felt that their traditional methods were superior.

But departure from traditional norms is never an impossibility, and where major fertility declines have taken place, such departure has often been an important factor. If couples lacking modern birth control methods are very determined to limit childbearing, they often manage to do so, whether by some folk method or through sexual abstinence. As mentioned elsewhere, U.S. fertility was very low during the economic depression of the 1930s, and for blacks as well as for whites, even though birth control methods were not easy to come by, and the methods preferred today were not yet available.

But couples who have wanted to limit births have often welcomed methods that are less restrictive on their sexual activity and convenience and that are more sure of success. Devices that might be considered prototypes of the condom were in use in Europe well before 1800, but the invention in the mid-1800s of modern-style condoms and diaphragms were a blessing to those who learned of them and had access to them. One might say that these were "just what they had been waiting for", and they were instrumental in the substantial fertility decline that began in western Europe about that time.

Much later breakthroughs were the advents of the contraceptive pill and intrauterine device (IUD) about 1960, and also the easier techniques of performing male and female sterilizations. But contraceptive sterilization had been practiced for many years.

Other Factors Affecting Fertility

Middle-class women were having sterilization operations as long ago as 1900. My own mother had the operation after her second child (my brother) was born.

In Europe celibacy was common because many young people became priests and nuns, and the custom of primogeniture also tended to prevent marriage or postpone it. The industrial revolution at first tended to raise fertility, because younger sons who could not inherit land could now get jobs in the city.

I have also not specifically mentioned family income or wealth among the factors leading to fertility reduction. Everyone knows the old saying that "the rich get richer and the poor get children", and in most societies lower-income people do indeed seem to have the most children. But income and wealth generally operate through one or more of the factors already discussed. Wealthier families are able to provide better health care for their children and so they see lower child mortality in their own and their friends' families. They are better educated and want to provide good education for their own children; they tend to be less traditional and may be less religious; and so on.

Yet it does not necessarily follow that their wealth is a compelling factor. In Arab countries, fertility is generally high, but in the oil-rich Arab countries it is even higher than in poorer countries like Egypt and Tunisia. Kuwait, before its invasion by Iraq, had almost the world's highest per capita GNP, and it also had a generous welfare system which provided a high living standard among all Kuwaiti families; yet Kuwait fertility remained high. Both in advanced and developing countries, whenever wealthy people want large families, they have them, but middle-income people who may also like the idea of having many children, nevertheless feel constrained to limit their fertility and to use whatever birth control methods are available.

Birth control methods in LDCs

When American and European population specialists turned their attention to the problem of LDC population growth, many made the mistake of believing that Western birth control methods would be eagerly accepted and fertility quickly decline. But there were several reasons why this did not happen.

World Population Growth

1. There was nationalist and political opposition. National pride can become offended if people think that their numbers might be cut down by outsiders. This is a factor in Latin America, where U.S. imperialism is resented. It is a factor in Africa also; Africans are suspicious from colonial days of white attitudes of superiority.

2. There was no concern about overpopulation, nor was there any understanding that the relation of number of children to number of workers would give rise to economic disadvantage.

3. People have what appear to them to be perfectly valid reasons for continuing to have large families. Some of these reasons seem so valid that they are favorably publicized in articles and books by reputable authors, such as the book by Mamdani already mentioned.

4. There was a fear or dislike of contraceptive methods. Women feared that the IUD and the Pill would have adverse health effects, and often their fears had some justification. Some Indian women using the IUD suffered excessive pain and bleeding. Their bad experience with the IUD impelled the Indian health authorities to forbid the use of the Pill in the Indian family planning program, even though the Pill was less likely to have had bad health effects.

The injectable steroid called Depo Provera had very successful use in Thailand, but it was banned in several other countries because it became known that it was not approved for use in the United States.

The condom is unpopular in many LDCs, partly because of the male machismo attitude, and partly because its use is associated with male relations with prostitutes. Sterilization is feared because it is surgical, and male sterilization is particularly opposed among ethnic groups — Latins, Africans, Muslims — who have a strong sense of male pride in procreation of children.

5. Quite aside from other objections is the attitude that birth control is immoral. Also men fear that birth control encourages women to be unfaithful. In many societies married women are indeed promiscuous, and some tragic events have occurred when men have had vasectomies and their wives subsequently became pregnant, even though the cause may have been failure of the vasectomy procedure.

6. People in many LDCs countries are satisfied with the folk methods of birth control that have been used for centuries, even though the methods may be quite ineffective.

7. There was lack of government commitment to family planning programs. Even when a government approved a family planning program, it had higher priorities elsewhere, and therefore failed to devote the effort to make the program effective.

But government-supported family planning programs have been remarkably effective in several LDCs. Though India's program proceeded very slowly for many years after its adoption, Indonesia's program, which started much later, has proceeded much more rapidly. The program is succeeding despite the fact that much of Indonesia consists of islands far distant from the capital (Jakarta in Java), and despite the fact that most of the population is Muslim.

Some factors that aided the Indonesian program were the development of an effective health infrastructure, the economic advances due to international demand for Indonesian oil. Also various attitudinal changes took have taken place in Indonesian culture, such as a rising regard for women and the realization of parents that "quality is more important than quantity" if children are to be prepared for a life better than what the parents themselves knew.

Contraceptive technology

Are more effective and more user-friendly contraceptives needed? Some authorities feel that they would be of great help, that there should be a male contraceptive pill, for example. Norplant, which when injected in a woman's arm prevents pregnancy for five years, was hailed as the miracle contraceptive, but we find now that it has its complications.

Certainly, female methods should be freer from health hazards and discomfort risks than they now are. If more men would use condoms or have vasectomies, family planning would have fewer complications. Not to mention the condom's protection from AIDS and other diseases.

World Population Growth

The best contraceptive technology
we'll ever have may be the condom

The condom was almost the only contraceptive option in the 1930s, when Americans urgently wanted small families and usually had them. The lack of better options today is less to blame for inadequate birth control than people's lack of commitment to have small families. Somebody once said that success in birth control requires "not the pill, but the will."

Chapter 12

Population Policies in Developing Countries

Is China's birth limitation policy so immoral?
— My question

My own work in the LDCs included the statistical evaluation of the family planning programs that were then in effect. In each of the countries where I was stationed, family planning comes under the government's health ministry. This is the case in almost LDCs, chiefly because family planning is best understood as a means to protect and improve the health of both mothers and babies.

India

Coming from the airport into downtown Bombay late one night in October 1968, I was amazed to see the crowds lining the streets. I had read that there were a quarter million sleepers on Bombay streets at nights, but it looked like more than a quarter million on our route alone. And here it was past midnight, and most of them — children included — were still awake.

In India I spent four years in population research and family planning evaluation under the auspices of USAID (the U.S. Agency for International Development). I had previously worked briefly in Colombia in 1966 and Nigeria in 1967. India's family planning project had started in 1952, but very little money was put into it by the Indian government, so it didn't get off the ground until 1966, when our government began funding it through USAID. The U.N. and some other governments also participated.

77

World Population Growth

India was the textbook case in the study of overpopulation. It was widely known as a huge and largely rural country which could not afford to feed, educate or properly house large numbers of its 500 million people. Today it has over 900 million people.

India's population is highly diversified as to language, religion, ethnicity, caste and culture. About 82 percent of its people are Hindus. Even though most of its original Muslim population are now in the new states Pakistan and Bangladesh, there are still over 100 million Muslims making up 12 percent of India's population. Besides Hindus and Muslims there are Christians (3 percent), Sikhs (2 percent), and fractional percentages of Jains, Parsis, Buddhists, Jews, etc. India's official language is Hindi, an Indo-European tongue derived from Sanskrit, but there are 13 other recognized languages.

Indians are so subdivided along language, religion and caste lines, that they usually tend to identify themselves by their various subdivisions rather than thinking of themselves as Indians.

Until the 1920s India's population grew very slowly. Even though birth rates were high, death rates were almost equally high because of recurring famines and epidemics. The death toll of the 1918-19 influenza epidemic was so great that the population was less in 1921 than it had been in 1911. The 1921 census showed 251 million people within India's present boundaries, and the population has grown almost fourfold since that date. As early as the 1930s, there was awareness of population pressure on India's land, but some Indians felt the problem could be solved by emigration to less crowded countries, notably Australia and the Americas.

The contraceptive methods in use in 1968 were vasectomies (male sterilizations), condoms and IUDs (intra-uterine devices). Oral contraception was strenuously opposed by Indian health authorities, and even now the Pill is not used in the family planning program. However, medical termination of pregnancy (i.e., abortion) was legalized in 1971. One of the legal grounds for its use was "contraceptive failure", and since this could neither be proved nor disproved, legal abortion became available virtually on demand.

Population Policies

In 1968, the family planning program was beginning to succeed but only in a few parts of the country. India's population was, and still is, largely rural. Illiteracy is still high in rural areas. Millions of women, on whose participation family planning largely depends, cannot even read a newspaper. The program was much more successful in the cities and in parts of the western and southern states than in the rest of India. It was less successful among Muslims than among Hindus and Sikhs, and most successful among Christians and the small Parsi community concentrated in Bombay.

Almost from the start, men were given incentives (cash or transistor radios) to accept vasectomy. During the years 1975-77, however, family planning became the pet project of Prime Minister Indira Gandhi's younger son Sanjay Gandhi, who pursued it zealously, so much so that the program became discredited in many quarters. Paid motivators were paid bounties to recruit vasectomy acceptors, and unwilling men were said to have been dragged into vasectomy camps, including men who were childless or had only one child. There was also experimentation with other forms of incentives and disincentives. For example, male government employees with two or more children were threatened with job loss if they didn't accept vasectomy.

Sanjay Gandhi's zeal enraged some of the electorate, and his mother was voted out of power in 1977. In 1980 she again became prime minister, only to lose her life by assassination in 1984. Meanwhile Sanjay was killed in a plane crash, and Indira's other son Rajiv became prime minister, also to be assassinated in 1989.

Many observers feel that Sanjay's zeal permanently damaged the Indian program. Yet the several million vasectomies performed in 1975-77 brought down the birth rate immediately, and also reduced significantly the number of people who would procreate children a generation later. Since 1977, however, female sterilizations have outnumbered male.

Almost all Asian cultures value sons far more than daughters, and this has been particularly true in India. A son is much more valuable than a daughter for support in old age. Also, when a daughter marries she becomes part of her husband's family. When a Hindu man dies, his son must officiate in the cremation service; if no son, then no proper salvation for the father's spirit. But even more important is the fact that most Hindu families are obliged to pay large dowries to marry off their daughters.

A family that has many daughters faces the risk of financial ruin, unless there are enough sons bringing dowry money into the family. For years female infanticide was practiced in north India, and even today girls are often neglected in food and health care, with the result that India is one of the few countries where female life expectancy is lower than male. Now that amniocentesis and ultrasound are available, a fetus found to be female is often aborted to avoid future dowry costs.

The relatively high fertility of Muslims crosses national boundaries. In every country where there are both Muslims and non-Muslims — India, Sri Lanka, Bangladesh, the Philippines, Syria — Muslim fertility distinctly exceeds non-Muslim. Muslim males, even more than Latin males, take a great pride in fatherhood.

In an earlier chapter I referred to our Muslim servant in Delhi, India. His wife gave him a total of nine children, two of whom died before he came to us. When we urged that he have a vasectomy to prevent additional pregnancies, he countered by telling us that his wife was having her ninth birth in a hospital and that she would have a tubectomy (female sterilization) there. But it turned out that the baby was born before she could get to the hospital. So again, we urged a vasectomy. He finally had one, despite the fact that all his Muslim friends urged him not to.

You will remember that I told of the marriage of his oldest daughter, a very beautiful and engaging young woman. A few years after her marriage, our former servant wrote to us (we were then no longer in India) that her Muslim husband had divorced her for her not having produced any children in the three years of their marriage. Our former servant and his family were very sad about the divorce.

But two years later came another letter, telling us that the daughter had married another man and had a child just a year later. What an embarrassment this must have been for her first husband!

Population Policies

China

During the early years of the Peoples Republic, population growth was not a matter of concern, since under Marxist doctrine overpopulation is a capitalist myth. The Chinese delegates at the 1974 population conference denounced the western nations' promotion of population control. But shortly afterward, China revealed a one-child policy far more drastic than any nation had ever considered.

Though China may originally have wanted its one-child policy to be nationwide, the policy operates today only in the major cities. Here is how I understand the policy: A newly marrying woman is asked to sign a pledge that she will have only one child; the signing is not mandatory, but the bureaucratic pressure is strong, and she usually signs. Later, if she becomes pregnant with a second child, she is called on to honor her pledge and have an abortion.

The Chinese, like the Indians and most other Asians, have a strong preference for sons. So if the first child was a boy, the woman and her husband usually consent to the abortion. But if the first was a girl, the parents may resist, and pressure is again brought into play. Although the woman is not supposed to be physically forced to have the abortion, there have been many cases where this has been done. At any rate, the whole policy has been called by many Americans, such as Pres. Reagan, a policy of "forced abortion", and has been strongly denounced.

Outside the major cities, the policy has been to permit two births, or sometimes even more. Since the cities where the one-child policy operates include not over 10 percent of China's population, China's total fertility rate is now about 2.0. This is below replacement level, but high enough so that population will continue to grow, as explained in the Demographic Appendix.

China's family planning program is not limited to abortion but includes sterilization and other contraceptive choices. By and large, the program works reasonably well. Many Chinese parents would prefer the large families prevalent in the past and may resent the current limitations, but reluctantly accept them.

The U.S. government should never have agreed to grant asylum to Chinese who claim that they seek it because of the birth limitation policy. Chinese people, like many millions of others,

81

seek to immigrate here, and find this asylum claim a convenient way to circumvent immigration restrictions. If they really want more than two children, we shouldn't want them.

Is China's birth limitation policy so immoral? The policy is only one of several steps that the Chinese government has taken to ward off famine and environmental degradation, and we should consider the policy both humane and responsible. If population growth in other countries is not brought under control within the next several decades, it is entirely likely that these countries may have to adopt even harsher policies than China's.

China should be applauded, rather than criticized, for not relying on other countries to provide its people living-space and income. In this respect, we can contrast it with Mexico, which counts on the United States to act as a safety-valve for its population growth. *Which policy is the more responsible?*

Latin America

Latin American countries were late in adopting family planning programs, both because they were slow in realizing that population growth might be a problem and also because of the powerful position of the Roman Catholic Church.

The Church in fact was effective for many years in maintaining prohibition against the importation and sale of contraceptive devices. Abortion was obviously prohibited also, but because contraception was usually unavailable, so many Latin American women resorted to abortion that in Chile and Peru abortions were at one time believed to outnumber live births.

I mentioned my own work in Colombia, where in 1966 I was asked to analyze a study of the frequency of abortion in the Popayan area. Here abortion prevalence was so high that local Catholic priests began to realize that contraception must be made available for the very purpose of reducing the abortion rate.

During the 1950s and 1960s, population growth rates were higher in Latin America than in other parts of the world (Africa has the highest growth rates today). Large families were the general rule. Female contraceptive methods were usually unavailable, and even though condoms were more often available, men seldom used them except with prostitutes.

Population Policies

Assistance to family planning programs were offered by USAID starting in the late 1960s. Although several Latin American governments accepted American assistance, local left-wing movements actively opposed them, denouncing them as genocidally motivated. Programs in Costa Rica, Colombia and Panama made considerable progress during the late 1960s and the 1970s. Each of these countries had total fertility rates of 6 or higher, but each one has now brought its TFR down to about 3. Argentina, Uruguay and Chile currently have TFRs below 3.

Until 1972, Mexico had a strongly pro-natalist policy. Even though contraceptives could legally be purchased through private sources, the government discouraged their use and prohibited their advertising. The total fertility rate during the years 1965-70 was close to 7. The opposition to birth control was more a result of government attitudes than it was the influence of the Catholic Church, which has little political power in Mexico. It is said that bishops in the Church expressed concern about Mexico's population growth even before the government did.

But in 1972 the government finally realized the seriousness of population growth, and reversed its policy against contraception. In 1974 it established a National Population Council, which took over the work of one of the non-governmental associations which had provided birth control assistance. By 1976, 50 hospitals and over 2,000 government health clinics were performing family planning services. By the mid-1980s the total fertility rate dropped to 4.2, and it is now estimated at 3.2.

However, because of the many recent years when fertility was very high, the number of women in their reproductive years is so large that the birth rate will probably continue at a high level for many years to come. As the Demographic Appendix will illustrate, even if fertility were to fall now to replacement level (about 2.2 in Mexico's case) and remain there, Mexico's population would rise — assuming no emigration — by over 60 percent before growth comes to a halt. From 3.2 to 2.2 would of itself be a major drop in TFR.

Mexican men — and Latin American men generally — have a reputation for "machismo", the form of male chauvinism in which men take pride in the number of children they have sired.

Mexican men nowadays deny that machismo exists, but on a visit in Mexico in 1977, I found that machismo was one of the things Mexican women talked most about. A woman sociologist told me that if it were up to Mexican women, there would be very few families with more than three children.

West Africa

Family planning had just been introduced in Nigeria under the sponsorship of the Ford Foundation when I arrived there in 1967. At that time, chief reliance was on IUDs (intrauterine contraceptive devices), and the campaign was advertised in newspapers and radio.

During the several weeks while I was there, a small but steady stream of women came to the clinic in Surelere (near Lagos) for insertion of the IUD. Most of these women were past 30 and had already had five or more children. My guess is that most of them were desperate to avoid future pregnancies, but they were also very afraid of what the IUDs would do to them. It soon became apparent that many of them had come to the clinic without their husbands' knowledge, and they may have been even more afraid of their husbands than of the IUDs.

Only about half of Nigerians are Muslim, and even among the non-Muslim population men are distinctly dominant and insist on complete authority over reproductive matters. The fact that a man has paid a bride price justifies that authority. The emotional tie a man has with his wife is much weaker than that with his paternal relatives, and they in turn expect him to have many children. The more children a man has, especially the more sons, the more his personal prestige.

Most West African governments approve family planning and recognize their population growth rate to be too high. Women as well as men know about contraception, but current use of modern methods, as estimated by surveys, is less than 5 percent in all West African countries except the Gambia. In Niger, a very primitive and landlocked country, almost half of the women know of modern contraceptive methods, but only 2 percent use them, mostly the Pill. Almost no West African men use condoms, which explains why so many African women are HIV-infected.

Population Policies

Sterilization

One of the major forms of birth control today is sterilization. The journal "Studies in Family Planning" reports the following figures as the percentages of married women whose form of birth control was sterilization, female or male, as of 1990:

	Female steril.%	Male steril.%	Total steril.%
More developed countries	7.6	3.8	11.4
East Asia	28.5	8.0	36.5
South Asia	16.0	4.8	20.8
Mid.East & North Africa	1.8	0.0	1.8
Sub-Saharan Africa	1.2	0.1	1.3
Latin America	21.0	0.6	21.6

Common as sterilization is in North America and Europe, it is even more resorted to in India, Sri Lanka, China and other Asian countries. I have already noted that male sterilization was an important form of birth control in India until the program was discredited under Sanjay Gandhi, after which female sterilizations exceeded male. In Sri Lanka most births take place in hospitals, and it is common for a mother to ask for sterilization immediately after her third or fourth childbirth. In South Korea, sterilization is as frequent a form of birth control as all other methods combined.

I like to look at the proportion of sterilizations elected by men as an index of male responsibility, the absence of machismo. In the United States and in some European countries, at least one-third of all sterilizations are male, whereas in Latin America and Muslim and African countries male sterilizations are very rare.

This is despite the fact that vasectomy, the male sterilization, is a very simple operation. In 1969 I saw it performed in a Bombay railroad station, where men lined up for it while waiting for their trains. The entire procedure, including all pre- and post-steps, took less than five minutes. Each man would then pick up his incentive money, walk off and board his train as if nothing unusual had happened. Tubectomy, the female procedure, is much more invasive and at that time was performed only in hospitals and was regarded as major surgery, though it has become simpler and safer today.

In Sri Lanka, incentive pay is offered to sterilization acceptors, either men or women, but the great majority are women.

One risk in vasectomy is that it has sometimes failed to sterilize. If a man has had the procedure and then his wife gets pregnant, you can imagine what the consequences might be. This risk itself has been known to discredit the operation.Whatever method men choose to use, the great need in family planning today is to increase male participation and responsibility.

Chapter 13

Sexuality and Childbearing in America

"There simply aren't any marriageable fellows around, so I might as well have a baby on my own."
— Attitude which some observers ascribe to young women to explain their having children out of wedlock

If you've read the preceding chapters, you may feel as I do that much of the procreation in the LDCs is irresponsible, in that little thought is given to the future welfare of the child. Are we much more responsible here in America?

One of the major concerns in the United States today is that of unwed childbearing. Those who express this concern do so in terms of teenage pregnancies. But it would be better to express concern for the children of unwed mothers, whether or not the mothers are teenagers. There are about 1.2 million such children born a year, and 70 percent of them are born to women in their 20s, 30s and 40s.

The sexual revolution

Almost any American who became an adult before World War II will have to agree that in matters of sexuality, things have changed almost beyond measure since the start of that war. The war itself brought millions of young men into the military, taking them far away from home communities where their activities were mostly known by their neighbors. The war threw them first into "basic training" or "boot" camps where they were deprived of usual companionship and where 90 percent of barracks talk was

on sex. Women as well as men were deprived of usual companionship. Women who had formerly stayed at home were now drawn
into jobs, and sometimes into war work far from home. For both
men and women, new opportunities for sexual activity presented
themselves. John Costello describes these changes in his book,
"Virtue Under Fire."

Not that all Americans were puritans before the war. There
had always been a fair amount of pre-marital and extra-marital
sex. Perhaps from a quarter to a half of young brides were pregnant when they marched down the aisle. But surveys made later,
such as Kinsey's, reported that at least 50 percent of American
women born before 1920 had neither married nor had sexual experience before their 20th birthday. Reports on teenage boys always show more early sexual activities than can be reconciled
with the reports on girls.

But the advent of the war, which ended American isola-
tion from world affairs, also ended the "age of innocence" in matters of sex.

Even within marriage, sexual activity must have been more
restrained during the 1930s than now. The economic depression
of the 1930's kept many couples in virtual desperation to mini-
mize childbearing, for even those who had jobs were uncertain as
to how long they could keep them. Birth control was not easy to
come by; condoms and diaphragms were available, but movement
of contraceptives in interstate commerce was technically illegal
under Federal law until 1936, and their sale was outlawed in some
states. Some of this illegality was circumvented by packaging condoms with the instruction, "For prevention of disease only."

Prior to the war, the long-term trends were later marriages
and decreasing fertility. The economic depression continued these
trends. The number of marriages fell to as low as one million a
year early in the 1930s, births to as low as two million a year.
Immediately after the war, marriages and births rose sharply to
make up for their postponement during both the depression and
war years.

Birth rates and births continued to rise almost to the end
of the 1950s. The years 1957 and 1958 were the peak years of the
"baby boom", with more than 4 million births a year. Marriages
happened earlier and it appeared that most couples wanted four
children. Sex was discussed in the media more than it had been

before. It became apparent that sexual activity increased even within marriage. At the same time, despite the increased proportions marrying, the rate of illegitimacy also increased.

The contraceptive revolution

At that point, no expansion had occurred in birth control technology. Abortion was illegal in all states except to save the life of the prospective mother, though it was performed with substantial yet unmeasured frequency, often disabling and even killing women.

In 1960, however, the birth control pill came into being and widespread use. Different varieties of IUDs (intrauterine contraceptive devices) were developed. It was now easier than ever before to engage in sex without fear of pregnancy, and also without marriage. This "contraceptive revolution" accelerated the sexual revolution.

Late in the 1960s, several states amended old abortion laws by expanding on the reasons for which abortion might be performed. Then in 1973, the Supreme Court's Roe vs. Wade decision made abortion available virtually on demand through the first six months of pregnancy. Its legalization made the procedure both safe and inexpensive. Now, when all other birth control methods failed — or when they failed to be used — sex without childbearing appeared to be at hand for all women who wanted it.

But what about out-of-wedlock births? One would expect that they would now rarely occur. Instead, the annual number of births to unmarried women, rose from about 80,000 in the mid-1930s to about 220,000 in 1960 and passed a million in 1988. In 1991, it was 1.2 million, over 25 percent of total births. Two important factors must be taken into account in considering it.

The changing marital scene

Prior to the 1940s young women who found themselves pre-maritally pregnant often managed to marry before childbirth; the proportion of brides pregnant at marriage may have been as high as one-half. Today many pregnant women do not wish to marry. Some have planned their pregnancies without any thought of marriage. Whether pregnant or not, much smaller proportions of young people are marrying. The following are comparative percentages, drawn from successive censuses:

World Population Growth

Proportions of persons currently married

	Female				Male			
	15-19	20-24	25-29	30-34	15-19	20-24	25-29	30-34
1930	12.6%	51.6%	74.9%	81.6%	1.7%	28.1%	61.3%	76.0%
1940	11.6	51.3	74.1	80.4	1.7	27.4	62.7	77.2
1950	16.7	65.6	83.3	86.2	3.1	39.9	74.2	84.3
1960	15.7	69.5	86.2	88.7	3.8	45.8	77.2	85.6
1970	11.3	60.5	82.5	86.1	3.9	42.9	77.1	85.7
1980	8.4	44.4	68.8	77.3	2.7	29.5	61.1	76.3
1990	5.2	32.1	59.5	69.6	2.2	19.7	48.3	64.6

You can see that the peak in the proportions married was reached about 1960 and after that came a sharp and continuing decline. The decline has been the result of two factors, a decreasing marriage rate and an increasing divorce rate.

The marriage rate decrease was not marked until the 1980s, but for years divorce has been steadily on the increase, even during the period when the marriage rate was increasing. Consider the following percentage distributions of women at ages 30-34:

	1930	1990
Never married	13.2%	18.3%
Currently married	81.6	69.6
Widowed	3.3	0.7
Divorced	1.9	11.4

But even these figures don't tell the whole story of women in the 30-34 age group. For one thing, of the women shown as married in 1990, 4.0 of the 69.6 were not living with their husbands (we do not know how many in 1930, but probably less than 4.0). Of the 65.6 who were living with their husbands, probably as many as one-tenth were in a second marriage.

In 1990 there were an estimated 3 million unwed couples sharing the same living quarters, and if these 6 million persons were counted as married, some of the 1990 percentages in the above tables would be quite different. For example, the percentage married among females at ages 20-24 would be about 38 percent instead of only 32 percent.

American Sexuality and Childbearing

Babies are born, whether women are married or not. The Demographic Appendix includes a table of age-specific fertility rates for years from the 1920s through the year 1990. These are composite rates for all marital status combined. If we compare recent rates with those of 1955-59 (the peak of the baby boom), we will note that the rates have declined even for ages under 25, and this would appear to validate the explanation that the increase in out-of-wedlock childbearing has been due to the decrease in the proportion of young women who are married.

But we might regard the baby boom as an aberration in the long-term trend, and look back to the situation of the 1920s and 1930s as the base line with which to compare present conditions. The age-specific rates are as high for young women now as they were then. We can very validly question why modern birth control has not reduced the fertility of young women, when it has so drastically reduced the fertility of women past age 25.

Yes, we know that adolescent sexual activity has greatly increased over the past 50 years. But is it biologically compelling for young women to bear children and for young men to sire them, whether or not they're married, and whether or not effective and legal birth control is available? Wouldn't it have been reasonable to expect that today's far more accessible contraception and abortion would have more than compensated for the increase in sexual activity? Isn't it clear that sexuality and procreation have become far less responsible than before?

And why are we concerned only with teenage unwed pregnancy? Out-of-wedlock births to women in their 20s are about 55 percent of total out-of-wedlock births. About 15 percent are births to women at ages 30 and over, despite the fact that only a relative minority of women at these ages are unmarried.

Yet it is births to teenagers that are the most talked about. Eighty percent of women reaching age 20 today are already sexually active, and teenagers tend not to use contraception in their initial sexual experiences.

The age at first sex activity has been getting younger and younger, possibly even more for boys than for girls. Some cities have adopted plans to distribute free condoms in high schools. But there are reports that boys are starting sexual activity as young as age 10. Many refuse to use condoms. Some compete with each other to see who can first get a girl pregnant. Some junior high girls I tutor tell me that their concerns are about AIDS, not about pregnancy.

While the proportion of out-of-wedlock births is much higher among blacks (68 percent in 1991) than among whites (22 percent), the actual number of white out-of-wedlock births is higher than that of black. The number of white has also been growing faster than the number of black, and has been growing particularly fast among high-income whites.

As noted, adult women now account for 70 percent of out-of- wedlock births. As they certainly know how not to have a baby, their pregnancies are often intentional. Just as pre-marital sex is no longer considered sinful, the stigma of out-of-wedlock childbearing has virtually disappeared — as has the very word "illegitimate."

Much of the today's unwed childbearing is blamed on poverty and the joblessness which prevents young men, especially blacks, from marrying. The much greater joblessness of the 1930s also prevented young people from marrying, but it didn't result in unwed childbearing. Today non-marriage is indeed more prevalent than ever before, and more prevalent among blacks than among whites. The 1990 census shows that the percentages of black women under age 35 who are married and living with their husbands are only about one-half of the corresponding percentages of white women.

*Easy sex, rather than joblessness,
is the main reason for non-marriage*

Joblessness is only one of the reasons for the present extent of non-marriage. The high rates of homicide and incarceration, especially of black men, are additional reasons. But the main reason is that marriage has gone out of fashion for many males because of easier availability of sex without marriage. Men with relatively high incomes, both white and black, are choosing to remain single, often because they are living with women to whom they are not married, or else preferring to maintain sexual relations with a number of partners without commitment to any of them.

American Sexuality and Childbearing

Though it is claimed that this non-marriage has caused most unwed childbearing, the rise of out-of-wedlock births started during the 1940s and 1950s, a period when employment and marriage of young people — blacks as well as whites — were on the increase. Also, the proportion of out-of-wedlock births continued rising after 1960 when modern birth control methods and then legal abortions became easily available.

The argument that teenage pregnancy is due to male joblessness is particularly weak when you note how many of the babies are fathered by teenage males, few of whom would have married even under the best of economic conditions. In 40 percent of recent births where the mother is under 20 and where birth certificates show the father's age, the father is shown to be under 20 himself.

Women's options

Can non-marriage of itself make unwed childbearing a young woman's rational choice? If she really hopes to marry eventually, and if marriageable males are scarce, that very scarcity should of itself deter her from childbearing, because being burdened with children will make that scarce husband even scarcer.

We are being told so often that disadvantaged women feel that the doors which might close to them because of childbearing are closed to them already. That they see no role open to them other than motherhood. We also hear that women want a child because they want someone to love them. But even if they see no cost to themselves in bearing children, they should be counseled to recognize the devastating cost to their children. They should be made to learn that the children they bear now are going to have a much poorer chance to leave the ghetto than the children they could have later if they don't bear children now.

Is it love to bear a child before
you're ready to provide the child
ample opportunity for a good life?

Dan Quayle and others have pointed this out in their remarks on family values. They note that there are unmarried women, even with high incomes, and more often white than black, who

93

purposely bear children without any intent to marry. They may feel that they can adequately provide for the children. But is it fair to a child to raise her or him without a husband present? If the child's parents do not have enough commitment to each other to marry, does either of them have commitment to the child?

The role of welfare

Has welfare induced unmarried women to bear children they wouldn't otherwise have had?

Sometimes. Welfare benefits, even when coupled with food stamps and Medicaid, are so small that bearing children is not a rational choice. But the awareness that welfare is out there, has certainly allowed unmarried women to be reckless in matters of sex and birth control. Also, the availability of welfare has often led them to keep their children instead of putting them up for adoption, to bring up the children themselves rather than moving in with their parents, and not to try to marry.

Aid to Families with Dependent Children (AFDC), didn't exist until after passage of the Social Security Act in 1935. Even then it was not designed for children born out-of-wedlock but was primarily a transitional provision for children of deceased, disabled or unemployed parents — children who would be receiving insurance benefits under the social security system as that system matured. In fact, Aid to Dependent Children, as it was then called, was hardly meant for newborn children at all, but instead for children who became dependent in the years following birth as the result of events such as orphanhood.

One reading the report of the Committee on Economic Security, which wrote the Social Security Act, won't find anything that would make it easier for persons to decide to have children they wouldn't otherwise have. The Social Security Act was passed in a decade when most people felt that neither they nor others should have children until they could afford them. During the 1930s there were other forms of welfare payments to impoverished families, mostly in the form of unemployment relief. Generally the small amounts paid were unrelated to the size of the family or the number of children. Married couples receiving these payments were nothing short of desperate in seeking to avoid having additional children. Today's women who go on welfare when a first child is born often continue childbearing while still on welfare.

For these reasons, I cannot agree with those who insist that the availability of welfare has no effect on childbearing. Welfare mothers I have known have told me that welfare played a major role in their deciding whether to have, or to keep, their babies.

But what about the various "reform" plans which would terminate welfare payments after two years and require welfare mothers to get jobs? No matter what we may think about mothers' irresponsibility in childbearing, our first concern must be for the children. Young children usually need their mothers to be at home with them. Unless we have much better employment opportunities than we now do, most of the reform proposals would do little good.

Moreover, they would save little money. The money spent out for AFDC, food stamps and Medicaid for the AFDC children and their mothers, is but a small percent of our GNP. Its cost is, for that matter, only a small percent of the total cost of all our income transfers and welfare programs, some of which (farm subsidies, for example) are for the benefit of wealthy people. Moreover, the money cost of benefits to children and mothers is certainly much less than the social cost of these children's births and of the malaise resulting from welfare dependence.

A much desired change, and one which would undoubtedly be a saving in both money cost and social cost, would be repeal of the Hyde Amendment, which compels poor women to bear children against their will.

If we cannot prevent males from fathering out-of-wedlock children, we must require child support from those who do. The Family Support Act of 1988 has brought in more support money than before, but too many unwed mothers refuse to identify the fathers of their children, and little has been done to implement the paternity tests permitted by the Act.

As I have mentioned, the social costs of unmarried parenthood far exceed the mere money costs. Much has been written about the handicaps of the unmarried mother in impaired education and career opportunities, but the effects on her children in terms of health, education and failure to rise out of poverty are still greater. Elsewhere I discuss the much greater infant mortality of children born out of wedlock, and it has been pointed out that these children are more likely to parent out-of-wedlock children and so perpetuate a cycle of poverty and welfare dependency.

For these and other reasons, it is so important to impress unmarried women with the fact that if they really love children, they will not bear them until they have first made adequate preparation to do so, including achieving a secure marriage.

The birth control issue

One of today's controversial issues is whether contraceptives should be made readily available and without cost to teenagers and whether instruction should be given in their use. Or, for that matter, whether children should receive sex education at school. Those religious groups which oppose sex education and birth control instruction outside the home, claim that these encourage sexual experimentation by teenagers who otherwise would refrain from sex. While their fear may have some validity, most studies show that teenage sex activity will go on with or without sex education, and that the net effect of such instruction is to reduce teen pregnancy.

It nevertheless seems regrettable that we live in a world where we have to instruct even young schoolchildren in such "facts of life" as sexual activity, birth control, "safe sex" and the avoidance of sexually transmitted diseases, including AIDS. It also seems regrettable that abortion, rape, and "gays" are in daily conversation and in the headlines of popular magazines displayed in the supermarket. Or that young people carry guns. Many of us older Americans would prefer a society free from the temptations and criminal influences that necessitate warning children at such early ages, and wish that young children could enjoy the carefree innocence of our own childhood.

However, unless conditions of society are improved, it is definitely better that children be protected against sexual hazards, and even with the help of public instruction to make up for insufficient instruction in the home.

American Sexuality and Childbearing

The "underclass"

Sociologists and social workers refer to an "underclass" which they define in various ways. I would suggest redefining the underclass as consisting of communities in which most members — young adults as well as children — were either born out of wedlock or brought up in broken families. It is in these households that we have by far the deepest poverty, the highest rates of school dropouts, of drug abuse and of violent crime. This underclass is as much white as it is black. Child poverty has greatly increased over the last 15 years. While some poverty exists in two-parent families because of depressed wages and increased unemployment, studies show that the major increase of child poverty since 1980 has been due to the great rise of single-parent families. On average, the condition of children in two-parent families has actually improved. About half of the black population now under age 30, as well as over one-tenth of the white, were born out of wedlock, and many who were born of married parents have experienced the divorce or separation of those parents. Divorces and separations and unwed parenting are less frequent in middle-class communities, but when divorces do occur in middle-income families, the divorced mother and her children often fall below the poverty line.

We can provide better for the
children already here if there
are fewer future births

The 1.2 million children being born out of wedlock annually must constitute a substantial share of America's poor children. The most important step that can be taken to reduce poverty in the United States is to prevent out-of-wedlock births. To do this we must persuade unmarried women not only to avoid pregnancy. We must impress upon them that it is unloving to bear a child until they have built their own lives to the point that they can enter a secure marriage. If the woman has been born into poverty herself, or born to a single mother, how can she want her child to be born into the same circumstance?

We have seen how AFDC has reduced the former financial deterrent against unwed parenthood and society has removed the social stigma. To counter these conditions, financial incentives are in operation or have been proposed to reward teenage girls to avoid pregnancy — or to avoid a second pregnancy if a child has already been born. Isabel Sawhill of the Urban Institute proposed a plan rewarding low-income teenagers (boys as well as girls) $5,000 vouchers for college or job training provided the teenager has finished high school without bearing or fathering a child.

But such proposals run into considerable opposition. Anti-abortion people fear that more pregnant young women would seek abortions. Some black leaders would fear a significant reduction of the black birth rate, since almost a quarter of all black births are those to teenage girls. (Such persons overlook the facts that white as well as black teenage births would be reduced, and that the births not occurring to teenagers would be replaced by later births under more favorable circumstances.)

On the other hand, it is certain that a plan like this would, in money terms, reduce AFDC costs by more than its own cash outlay, because each birth to a teenager would cost many times more than the cash award to non-bearers, even though the latter would be more numerous. Even more important than the money saved would be the improved lives of the teenagers themselves and of the children whom they would bear later as adults. It might even lead many young people to resist pressures to initiate sexual activity.

Other suggestions are even more drastic and controversial. I have commented that the great dilemma over welfare is whether we can protect children without rewarding the irresponsibility of their parents. Alice Griffin, a black New York attorney writing in the New York Times of March 13, 1991, urges that children born to teenage mothers be taken from them and placed in institutions or homes where they could be raised properly and in a favorable environment. The mothers would be denied AFDC payments, though they could receive temporary assistance while working or continuing in school. Ms. Griffin recognizes that the real victims of teenage pregnancy are the offspring and that they cannot "be successfully raised in ghettos so long as their mothers receive public assistance." She also claims that in a scenario where

AFDC payments are denied and babies are removed from the custody of teenage mothers, teenagers would have every incentive to avoid pregnancy.

Ever since Norplant (the steroid injected in the arm to prevent pregnancy for five years) has become available here, there have been proposals to require welfare mothers to be injected with it. Such form of compulsion is wrong and a poor substitute for education. It is to be hoped, however, that Norplant may become available at low cost (or without cost) to low-income women for voluntary use.

But society may be driven to such forms of compulsion at a future date. We must remember that if society has an obligation to support every child born in this country, society must also have some say as to how many children any mother be allowed to bear.

Also, we could do far more for the poor children already born, if we could slow down the entry of new children into the poverty ranks.

Our oversexed society

I have referred to the non-use of birth control in American sexual activity, especially the refusal of young sexually active males to use condoms. But birth control would treat only the symptoms, not the fundamental situation. Whatever could lead our society to be less sex-driven would be all to the good. Sexual urge is greatly over-stimulated by open discussion of sexual matters in newspapers, magazines and advertising in general. There is an increasing degree of sex portrayal in movies and television. The "soap operas" viewed daily by millions of Americans and the magazines and paperback books displayed at the supermarket portray sexual promiscuity and marital infidelity as normal life styles.

I have noted that sexual excesses and unwed childbearing are on the increase in the LDCs as well as here, and I am sure that American movies and TV dramas have contributed to this increase.

Unwed childbearing, domestic violence, rape,
child abuse, divorce, even poverty itself, can
be laid to society's obsession with sex.

World Population Growth

The increased "sex consciousness" of recent decades is very likely the basis for the great and increasing number of sex crimes in our society, such as forcible rape and sexual abuse of children. To illustrate the effect of today's sexual permissiveness, consider the frequency of "date rape", which can be explained by the male attitude that since most young women are non-virgin anyhow, an additional sexual encounter won't hurt them.

In a less violent but equally tragic area, our preoccupation with sex has disturbed the stability of American marriages; the demand for sex satisfaction and the belief that it can more easily be found outside of one's present marriage is obviously a major factor leading to divorce, with consequent damage to the lives of children.

I'm not so naive as to argue against sex. Sex is one of the most satisfying experience of human beings, and it's here to stay. To some degree, the more liberal sexual conventions of today may be helpful, and pre-marital sexual abstinence in the face of today's sexual stimuli and late-marriage trend may be impossible for many people. But our society, perhaps more than any other, has gone overboard in its preoccupation, its obsession, with everything pertaining to sex. Sex is indeed delicious, but like almost everything delicious, it can cause a lot of indigestion, and in fact it has soured many aspects of modern life. And one of its most tragic effects, an effect that is avoidable, is unwed parenting.

How can we return to less destructive sexual behavior? Certainly not by throwing out sex education or by limiting it to the mere preaching of abstinence. Or even by talking "family values." Yet somehow, women must come to realize that the fun of casual sex is outweighed by its hazards and heartbreaks, and that men are unwilling to marry or even enter a committed non-marital relationship so long as there is no need for commitment.

The problem is certainly not confined to the United States. The sexual revolution is worldwide in one degree or another. The Islamic protests at Cairo over sexual permissiveness suggest the possibility that permissiveness has come to Islamic countries also. Unwed parenting is even more common in northern Europe than here. In Sweden, fully 50 percent of births are out-of-wedlock, though it is believed that the unwed unions there are much more permanent than ours and involve far more paternal responsibility. Unwed childbearing is also very common in Latin America.

American Sexuality and Childbearing

The abortion controversy

As was conceded at the Cairo Conference, abortion cannot be viewed as a correct form of birth control. The great majority of the 1.5 million abortions performed here each year could have been prevented by responsible sexual behavior. *But women must not be compelled against their will to carry a pregnancy to term or to undergo childbirth.* Abortion must also be available without cost to poor women.

Anti-abortion demonstrators have discredited their own cause by their overzealous and violent conduct. I have heard male demonstrators say of women seeking abortion, "If she didn't want a baby, she shouldn't have had sex." How many of these men have had sex without wanting the full responsibilities of parenthood?

But we must recognize that irresponsible sexuality is of itself an issue. If those who insist on abortion rights were equally concerned over the number of people who engage in sex recklessly and then resort to abortion, freedom to choose abortion would be under far less attack than it now is.

There are certainly many Americans of good will who feel that abortion should be illegal. But it is unfortunate that they do not understand the many personal tragedies that would occur if abortion were again prohibited — tragedies against the welfare of both women and children. They also lose sight of the fact that *if there were no unwanted pregnancies, there could be no abortions.*

The adoption alternative

Certainly, it would be a blessing if most of the children who now live in fatherless homes, or who are shifted in and out of foster homes, could be adopted into secure families. Couples who are unable to have babies of their own, could do better by adopting babies born in our own country than either going through costly infertility treatments or going abroad to adopt children.

But for the woman who finds herself in an unwanted pregnancy, arranging for adoption isn't always an adequate alternative to abortion. Should she be denied the right to abortion just because there may be couples who would want to adopt her child? She could well ask: "Why should I have to go through months of discomfort, possibly having to give up my schooling or job as well, followed by the pain of childbirth, just to be the incubator for a child I may never see again?" Especially when the man who sired the child goes free of all cost, discomfort and pain, and may even have walked out on her, possibly unaware of the pregnancy he has caused?

There are 1.2 million out-of-wedlock births in the United States every year, but probably not over 50,000 legal adoptions take place annually, not counting adoptions by relatives of the unwed mother. We know that many white unmarried women purposely bear children they wish to bring up, that some girls are persuaded by their parents to keep their babies rather than to offer them for adoption, and that the availability of welfare money helps women keep their babies. But there must be many women who keep their babies only because they see no prospects of their babies being adopted. This is particularly true of black women. There is no evidence that pro-life activists go out of their way either to adopt black babies or to assure the large amounts of money a black mother needs if she is to raise her baby with the same advantages as a middle-class white child would have.

But it should be noted that some blacks oppose the idea of interracial adoption. The National Association of Black Social Workers has stated that, "Black children in white homes are cut off from the healthy development of themselves as Black people." Blacks also fear that a black child raised in a white family would not be taught the "black survival skills" that help him face discrimination. Regardless of such concerns, isn't it better that a child be welcomed into a loving white home than to continue to be homeless? And isn't there a positive race-relations effect when children of different races grow up in the same family?

Blaming the victim?

Isn't it sad that those who express great concern about the plight of disadvantaged children, nevertheless keep silent about the irresponsibility of bearing children into obvious conditions of disadvantage and poverty? The late Michael Harrington pleaded passionately on behalf of poor families, but he could see nothing wrong in thoughtless and unrestricted childbearing. In the August 25, 1964 issue of *Look,* he described, with pictures, the miserable situation of a white family with seven children living in a Boston slum. He was obviously seeking sympathy for the parents, claiming that society had victimized them by letting them be so poor.

In a subsequent issue of the magazine, one reader responded by expressing sympathy for the children but scorn for the parents' irresponsibility in having more children than they could support. Another reader pointed out how Catholic teachings against birth control had contributed to the family's misery.

Mother Theresa won the Nobel Peace Prize for her compassionate work among India's poor. But in her support for Catholic teachings, she has refused to recognize how irresponsible childbearing has compounded Indian poverty. Today Harrington is still revered as a great friend of the American poor, though he too failed to see how Catholic teachings contributed to the misery of poor families.

The various child advocacy organizations recognize the handicap in which a teenage woman places herself when she bears a child. Some have the unfortunate tendency, however, to insist that the woman must not be criticized if she is poor, and to excuse her on the ground that she is a victim of society. If we really desire to reduce poverty, why should we be reluctant to acknowledge that irresponsible childbearing is a crime against children and an act which tends to perpetuate an impoverished underclass?

Poverty may be an explanation, but it is not an excuse for bearing babies into a life of handicap and disadvantage. The women who do this know what they are doing, though they may not fully realize how unloving their behavior is. *They are not the victims; their babies are.* Isn't it time to recognize irresponsible childbearing for what it is, and to stop excusing it?

Chapter 14

Other Demographic Factors

"There is neither Jew nor Greek ... bond nor free ... male nor female, but ... fellow citizens ... of the household of God."
—Paul (Galatians 3:28, Ephesians 2:19)

Age

You have already noted the variation in age structure of different populations. In the U.S. population 13 percent are age 65 or older, and 22 percent are under age 15. In Niger in West Africa, as another example, only 3 percent are 65 or older and 49 percent are under 15. Both high fertility and high mortality are responsible for Niger's typically-African age distribution. Not only are there many births per woman, but each year's births are usually greater in number than the births of the year before. Also a much lower proportion of people survive to the oldest ages.

Because fertility in many European countries has been lower than ours for some time, their proportion of young people is less than ours and their proportion of elderly people greater than ours. In Sweden the proportion under age 15 is 18 percent and the proportion 65 and over is also 18 percent.

The dependency ratio

Economists have sometimes referred to what they call the "dependency ratio", which is the ratio of the sum of these two proportions to the proportion at ages 15-64. For the United States, the dependency ratio would now be 35 percent (22 plus 13) divided by 65 percent, or .54. For Sweden it would be 36 (18 plus 18) divided by 64, or .56. For Niger it would be 52 (49 plus 3) divided by 48, or 1.08, about double the U.S. or Swedish ratios.

World Population Growth

The idea of the dependency ratio is that those at the youngest and oldest ages are economically dependent on the persons at ages 15-64. In theory, the higher the ratio, the worse off the country.

The ratio doesn't apply with equal force in all countries. In our country, young people are economically dependent well past age 15, particularly if they are supported by their parents while studying in college. In LDCs some boys under age 15 live away from home and are self-supporting, while others live at home and contribute economically to their families. Also, most Americans do not become dependent on their children at age 65, since many work beyond that age, and many of those not working own their own homes and live on pensions and on income from their investments. (Social security, however, is a form of dependency, since benefits for retired persons are paid for primarily by persons who are currently working.)

The dependency ratio is nevertheless viewed as a factor affecting a country's economy. Because Niger has a high dependency ratio, a larger proportion of the work performed by people at ages 15-64 is devoted to supporting others (feeding, caring, etc.), than would be the case if its dependency proportion were lower. Therefore, less of the work performed goes into the sort of saving that could advance the country economically.

Old-age dependency

As already noted, countries in North America and Europe have a relatively high proportion of people at the older ages, with the United States having 13 percent at ages 65 and over and some European countries even higher percentages. Sweden, as we saw, has 18 percent of its population past age 65. These percentages are almost certain to rise, even if mortality and fertility have little change. As you will see in the Demographic Appendix, the age distribution of a population whose TFR is close to replacement level, becomes closer and closer to that of the life table. In the United States, we might have as much as 20 percent of our population past age 65 by the year 2025, if in the intervening years we have low fertility and low immigration.

The problem with an increasing proportion of older people in the population is not only their income dependency in the usual

Other Demographic Factors

sense but also their substantial health care costs. If health care costs continue to rise, the total cost of keeping only elderly people alive and well might greatly exceed 20 percent of the nation's GNP.

This sounds like an argument in favor of high immigration and high fertility and against the greater use of contraception. But this is faulty thinking. It is true that most immigrants are now young and have high fertility, but immigrants will get old too. Unless they return to their original homelands when they get old, their income needs and health care costs will become part of ours. If they do return, their costs will burden their original homelands.

I have already commented that even though elderly people in the LDCs had hoped to receive support in old age from their sons, many are not receiving it. Having many children will not pay off if the world the children will live in will be so overpopulated that there will not be enough good jobs.

After all, population aging is a problem for the whole world. Moreover, world population is certain to stop growing some day, even if it reaches 20 billion before it stops. Whenever it does stop, it will be because fertility will have fallen to replacement level and remained at or below replacement level for many years. Unless mortality rises to such an extent that replacement level can be reached with relatively high fertility, a large proportion of elderly in the total world population is inevitable.

That being the case, wouldn't it be far better to slow down population growth as much as possible now? We could then face this old-age dependency problem in the near future, while world population is at a fairly tolerable level — say at 6 or 7 billion — than to have to face it when it reaches a much higher figure. If we let world population grow to a very high level, we will have had such drastic problems that we won't know how to face the additional problem of the high proportion of elderly people.

Sex differentials in birth and survival

In most countries slightly more boy babies are born than girls. There is some variation in the ratio; among U.S. whites, male births exceed female by about 6 percent, among U.S. blacks, about 3 percent. There may also be a slight variation according to the ages of the parents.

World Population Growth

In most advanced countries, the male probability of death now exceeds the female probability at every age. The result is that a female birth cohort, even though starting out several percent below a male cohort of the same birth year, will overtake the male cohort before age 50, and probably outnumber the male cohort by two-to-one before age 85. Male infant mortality (mortality at age 0) exceeds female by about 30 percent just from natural causes. In later childhood and in adult life, much but not all excess male mortality is due to injuries, since boys and men are physically more venturesome than girls and women, more likely to engage in dangerous sports and occupations, and in both military and civilian combat.

In LDCs, however, female mortality may exceed male, either due to poorer nutrition and health care of girls or due to maternal mortality during the reproductive ages. But even in such cases, a female birth cohort will usually overtake a male at some age. Also female life expectancy at birth usually exceeds male. India is one of the few countries where male life expectancy exceeds female.

Infant mortality

The infant mortality rate, the probability of death within the first year of life, varies greatly from country to country and has decreased rapidly over time. As noted in an earlier chapter, the U.S. infant mortality rate in 1930 was higher than the present rate in most LDCs, other than in Africa, and was over six times the present U.S. rate. Despite all the talk about how high U.S. infant mortality is, its present rate is really remarkably low.

Any baby's death, whether here or anywhere, is a tragedy. But would you call a 99 percent survival rate a failure? Out of every 1,000 U.S. babies born, 992 survive to their first birthday. That is admittedly not as good as Japan's 996 out of 1,000, or as good as the 995, 994 or 993 in several other advanced countries. Hopefully our survival rate will continue to improve, but meanwhile we should acknowledge that it has already improved a lot.

What is tragic in our country is the high number of cases where pregnant women receive little or no pre-natal care. Not all this lack of care is due to lack of health service. Statistics on pre-natal care visits suggest that many unmarried expectant mothers neglect care, showing the same recklessness that led to unwed pregnancy in the first place. In a health insurance meeting in Seattle, one physician said that our infant mortality is more a matter of life style than lack of health care.

Statistics show that infant mortality is lowest for babies born to women at ages 25-29. They also show that for any given age or race, infant mortality is at least 50 percent higher for babies born to unwed mothers than for babies born to married mothers. We should note, however, that it is poorer women who bear children at young ages and before marriage. There is much research to be done before we can measure the effect of each of the factors, maternal age, marital status and poverty. Black infant mortality is twice that of white partly due to a combination of these factors. But there may also be a genetic factor involved, similar to the factor that makes male infant mortality 30 percent greater than female.

Race or ethnicity

Many population data are subdivided by race, just as many are subdivided according to sex (gender) and age. Some are also subdivided according to religion, particularly in countries such as India where the two largest religious groups, Hindus and Muslims, are very different in fertility behavior even though they are of the same race.

In dealing with race, sex and age differences, we must remember that group differences are generally only differences between averages within the different groups and do not indicate that all individuals within one group differ in characteristics from those of another. Thus, if the average Math score of U.S. males taking the S.A.T. is 500 and the average for females is 480, this certainly does not mean that every male has a higher score than every female or that in any randomly chosen male-female pair the male has a higher score than the female.

TFRs (total fertility rates) are averages of the fertility of individuals. As averages, they differ widely between the various U.S. ethnic groups. TFRs calculated from age-specific fertility rates of 1990 were as follows:

Mexican/Cen. American	3.20	Non-Hispanic White	1.85
Non-Hispanic Black	2.52	Cuban-American	1.46
Native American	2.18	Chinese-American	1.36
Filipino-American	1.88	Japanese-American	1.11

Note the breadth of the range. The Mexican/Central-American rate is almost triple the Japanese-American, despite the fact that it is a composite of rates of women of Mexican ancestry born in the United States and immigrant women born in Mexico and Central America. An unofficial rate for the immigrant women is 3.9, which if correct is higher than the TFR of women in Mexico.

We do not have exactly the same race breakdowns for infant mortality. However, whites — both non-Hispanic and Hispanic —and also Native Americans have infant mortality rates in the range of 8 to 10 (per 1,000 live births), blacks have rates about double those of whites, and Asian-Americans have rates about half of whites. Again, Japanese-Americans have the lowest rate, less than 4.

At most older childhood ages and at adult ages also, black Americans have the highest mortality rates, suffering more from homicide, AIDS, hypertension and various other causes than do other ethnic groups.

To some extent, the various rates are affected by economic conditions prevailing among the different racial groups, but there are some differences not explained by economics. The proportion of Native Americans living below the poverty line is about the same as for blacks. Also the proportion of children born to unwed mothers is almost as high among Native Americans (53 percent) as among blacks (68 percent). Yet Native Americans have much lower infant mortality than blacks.

Numbers of children are a matter of choice among individuals and races. But when we note that low fertility tends to be associated with economic success, we have to ask which of the two is cause and which is effect. In the case of blacks, poverty and high fertility seem closely associated, though a closer correlation is that of low fertility with education; highly educated blacks are found to have very low fertility.

Official vital statistics do not identify Jews, but it is known that American Jews have both much lower fertility and also lower mortality rates than the general population. Though Jews may have had relatively high fertility while living in eastern Europe, their fertility has been remarkably low since coming to America. One sociologist has noted that the poorer a Jewish couple was, the more careful it was to maximize their children's advantages by procreating few of them. Another has written that birth control has been an engine of economic success for Jews.

One of the great disappointments of the 1990s is the fact that the social and economic divisions between African-American and non-Hispanic whites are still very wide, that neither residential segregation nor school segregation have disappeared. In fact, school segregation definitely worsened during the 1980s. Worst of all, hate crimes occur frequently in all parts of the country.

The National School Boards Association blames part of the worsening of school segregation on interracial differences in birth rates and on immigration. It implies that there needs to be more white children of school age if there is to be real integration. There is a basis for this argument. When the Supreme Court ruled against school segregation in 1954, about 85 percent of the U.S. child population at ages 5-17 were non-Hispanic white, in 1990 only 69 percent. In cities where immigrants and minorities are concentrated, non-Hispanic white children are a much smaller percent of the school-age population. Instead of 69 percent, we find only 32 percent in Los Angeles, only 11 percent in Washington, DC. We need larger percentages of whites than these for successful school integration.

During the 1960s, many Americans hoped that the civil rights movement would lead not only to the end of racial hatred and racial discrimination but even to the end of racial distinction. Just as the various European groups had melded in the American "melting pot", with intermarriage becoming more the rule than the exception, many of us had hoped that this would also be true even as between so-called races. I say "so-called", because we know that the great majority of blacks have some white ancestors and a sizable minority of whites have some black ancestors.

Unfortunately, it didn't work out as many of us had hoped. The initial fault was that of those members of the white majority who refused to accept the spirit of racial equality. Instead of welcoming the school desegregation decision and the civil rights legislation that followed it, large numbers of whites defied the reforms ordered by courts and Congress. White flight into the suburbs and enrollment of white children in private schools were part of this defiance.

There are two opposing factors at work in American society in response to the inevitable demographic changes. One is the tendency to focus attention on ethnic identity and to harden lines of division. This leads to fears and hopes as to which ethnic group can lose or acquire desired status and power.

The second is a growing degree of understanding and tolerance between groups. Fortunately, this is going on at a greater degree than we might imagine, thanks to the efforts of so many people of good will. How long it will take for this factor to prevail and bring about not only inter-ethnic harmony but also ethnic coalescence we cannot tell. But this should be our goal.

In other countries also, race distinctions are exaggerated or even unreal. In Sri Lanka, Tamils and Sinhalese have been fighting each other since independence from Britain, but anthropologists have proved that there is no genetic difference between the two groups. There has been so much intermarriage over the centuries that, even if there ever was any "racial" distinction, it has faded out. Those who are members of either group are members simply because some of their forbears chose to adopt the language and religion and other cultural attributes of that group.

The very same claim can be made with respect to the Croats, Serbs and Muslims in Bosnia. These groups differ by religion, not race, and this difference is mostly historical. Religion is no longer a factor in their lives. In Rwanda and Burundi, the "tall" Tutsis are not wholly distinct from the "short" Hutus.

More on poverty

Just how much of fertility differences can really be blamed on poverty? In our own country, fertility was very low during the depression of the 1930s, but then it rose during the 1940s and rose even higher during the 1950s, times which were considered very prosperous.

Religion may be more of a factor than race or poverty. The Hutterites, who are whites and whose fertility is extremely high, are a prosperous community. So are the Mormons, whose fertility is relatively high. In India, Muslims and Hindus are of the same race. But Muslim fertility is higher than Hindu, and it is commonly accepted that this is because Muslims are poorer on average than Hindus. But in Sri Lanka, where Muslims on average are wealthier than Hindus or Buddhists, Muslim fertility is again higher than either Hindu or Buddhist, and conspicuously high in the wealthy Muslim families.

Other Demographic Factors

In many societies, poverty acts as a restraint on fertility. This certainly was the case during the U.S. economic depression of the 1930s. But my observation is that it acts as a restraint even in LDCs when people are sufficiently aware of high fertility's cost. In Sri Lanka, where large families had always been regarded as an ideal and a blessing, people would almost invariably tell me that they wanted to have many children and that the reason for not having them was that they couldn't afford them.

One can call it poverty when LDC parents feel the need for sons to support them in old age, even though the sons may become unable to supply the expected support. But poverty is not a valid excuse for a woman, whether in an LDC or here at home, to bear one child after another when she knows that each new birth is going to add to the misery, disadvantage and hopelessness of all her children.

High fertility may not be the cause of poverty, but it often is one of the important factors which keeps individuals and groups from rising out of poverty. If the poor in any land can accept the idea of choosing small families, there is real reason for believing that they will raise themselves economically. But how much LDCs can raise themselves without massive transfer payments is uncertain. In the United States, even those of us who understand the poverty of the LDCs feel that we must first help our own poor.

The following chapter will tell of the great demand of LDC people to flee from the poverty and overcrowding of their home countries and come to North America, Europe or Australia. No conceivable amount of wealth transfer would suffice to make life bearable enough in some LDCs for people to be content to remain there.

But in our own country, there can be no excuse for not taking the comparatively simple and relatively inexpensive steps that would lessen poverty here and give new hope to our poorest children.

Chapter 15

Immigration

"Much as I detest the United States and its politics,
it doesn't stop me from wanting to live there."
—Comment of a Palestinian friend

How has immigration into the United States affected you, and how will it affect your children? Will the increased diversity which these immigrants bring enrich your children's lives? Or will their lives be made more difficult by increased overcrowding and increased competition for jobs?

New projections by the Census Bureau show that our population, instead of topping out at 300 million or less in the 21st century, may pass 450 million. The reasons for the change are the increased level of expected immigration and the high fertility of immigrants.

International migration was hardly discussed at all in the 1974 and 1984 population conferences. In 1974 the LDCs didn't want even to suggest that they might be overpopulated. In 1984 there was some discussion of the rights of those who had already settled in new countries. At the 1994 conference in Cairo, there were demands by some LDC delegations that North America, Europe and Australia admit increased numbers of immigrants, particularly family members of earlier immigrants. Nothing significant came of these demands.

There are two sharply opposing theories you should know about. One theory is that everybody in the world has the *right* to live in any country he chooses. One variation of this theory is that any country that has a low birth rate and is therefore relatively uncrowded, is morally obliged to accept all comers from a country that has a high birth rate and is more crowded. Some Roman Catholic churchmen have voiced this theory.

The second theory is that nobody in the world has the right to settle in a new country unless people in that new country choose to give him that right. In practice this means that every sovereign country has the right to exclude from its borders anyone it chooses to exclude. This is the theory held by most governments.

Those who support this second theory might well ask: "Why should a country whose people carefully control their own fertility have any obligation to relieve the overpopulation of countries whose people do not control their fertility?"

International migration has accelerated during recent decades to the point that an estimated 125 million persons are living outside of the countries of their birth. Most of this movement of people has taken place among the LDCs themselves. There have been great refugee movements, first of all within Africa itself, but also resulting from the invasion of Afghanistan by the Soviets, the Gulf War, and the dismemberment of the former Soviet Union and the former Yugoslavia. The most recent major displacement has been that of Rwandans. There has also been the movements of job seekers to the oil-producing countries of the Middle East. Millions of people were displaced by the Vietnam War. There are millions of people still living who were displaced during and immediately after World War II.

Is a country whose people control their fertility obliged to relieve the over-population of countries whose people do not control their fertility?

Population growth in the LDCs has had a major role in pushing people into the developed countries of North America and Europe. It would be difficult to determine how much of this migration would have taken place if LDC population growth had been less rapid. The greater wealth of the developed world, the increased communication which publicized that wealth, and the easier modes of transportation, all stimulated and facilitated the migration flow.

Moreover, immigration into a country breeds more immigration, since those who have already come seek to bring their relatives. Most governments have been willing to permit family reunification, though not to the extent that LDC delegations asked for in Cairo. Meanwhile, remittances flow to family members left behind. The economic problems of LDCs are relieved both by the import of remittances and by the export of people, relieving their overcrowding and unemployment.

The U.S. situation

The United States is said to be currently accepting for permanent settlement as many immigrants and refugees as all other countries combined. On the other hand, the 1990 census showed only 8 percent of U.S. residents to be foreign born, as opposed to over 20 percent both in Canada and in Australia. However, a much greater proportion of immigrants into the United States are from the developing countries.

Immigration, like abortion, is an issue on which many Americans have strong feelings. The abortion issue has large numbers on each side, but the immigration issue is more one-sided. There are some Americans who feel good about our present level of immigration, or who feel we should be even more generous. But they are far fewer than those who think immigration should be curtailed and illegal immigration stopped altogether. Some would say to other countries, "Don't send us your surplus people. We're too crowded for comfort already."

Border-crossing has become an international phenomenon. A million people enter our borders on a typical day. This of course includes daily commuters, visiting foreign tourists, returning American tourists, but also foreigners who have come to stay. Our legal immigration is running about one million a year. We do not know how many come and stay illegally, since they obviously cannot be counted. But there are certainly several million people residing here illegally (we use the term "undocumented aliens"). There are also people who emigrate permanently; we do not know the annual number, but it may be as high as 200,000.

World Population Growth

Millions of people in Latin America, Asia, and now Africa, even though they know of the U.S. crime rate, racism, unemployment, congested automobile traffic, and our many other problems, think of our country as the one in which they want to live. Our congested traffic may in fact be one of the biggest attractions, since they envy the fact that most of us drive our own cars.

They know also that we have far better jobs and higher earnings than they, that our work has greater dignity and less drudgery and fewer periods of unemployment. Having seen so much of our high living in movies and television, they are sure that when they arrive here they will share in that good life. In many cases they will also look forward to better personal development from the opportunities here, having heard of the success other immigrants have had. Even though many may dislike the political actions we have taken in their world, they also hope to enjoy greater political freedom here and also freedom from the many restraints in their home countries.

People must also be attracted to the United States because it is regarded as the world's most powerful country, the country least likely to be invaded by others, and therefore the country with the most security and the most prestige.

I wish I could include in this book some photos of scenes of Latin Americans, Asians and Africans thronging the U.S. embassies and consulates in the hope of getting visas of any kind to enter the United States. The crowds are so great that, until you realize that they are not carrying weapons, you might believe that our offices were under attack. I once had to visit a consular office in Accra, Ghana. Hundreds of educated Ghanaian young people had come that day in hopes of getting student visas. The consular officer told me that he had to turn many down, because even though they had admission papers and scholarship awards from U.S. colleges, he often sensed the likelihood that they would not even report to the college when they arrived here but would manage to "get lost" in our population.

I learned that black Americans who visit Africa run the risk of having their passports stolen. If the thief can't himself pass for the American pictured in the passport, he will find someone who can and will get a good price for it.

Immigration

There are many other ways of successfully getting around American immigration restrictions. Foreigners (of either sex) marry U.S. citizens for the primary purpose of getting a "green card" for permanent status. The INS (Immigration and Naturalization Service) contends that many such marriages are fraudulent. Foreign women, or couples, time their visits here so that their expected babies will be born here and therefore qualify for U.S. citizenship. The children can then stay here and make it hard for us to deport their mothers, or they can return here later to stay and sponsor their parents as immigrants. For U.S. immigration laws not only give preference to relatives of persons already here, but also exempt many categories from numerical quotas and limits altogether. At present, large numbers of people are circumventing regular immigration channels by simply entering the country, either illegally or on a temporary visa, and then claiming political asylum.

Immigration then and now

Until the 1960s, most immigrants were Europeans, and up to about 1880, most of them were from northern and western Europe, from Britain, Ireland, Germany, the low countries and Scandinavia. Relatively few were from France, a less crowded country with slower population growth. For many years after 1880 the majority were from southern and eastern Europe, from Italy, the Balkans, Russia and Poland (which was then included in Russia). The quotas in effect from the 1920s until the 1960s restricted immigration from southern and eastern Europe and favored northern and western. Sometimes not enough north or west Europeans came to fill their quotas. Also, during the late 1800s we had immigrants from China and Japan. Later, Asian immigration was later virtually shut off. And all along we had immigrants from Mexico. We had also absorbed the Mexicans who lived in the southwestern areas we had acquired from Mexico.

World Population Growth

The following data show the changing sources of our immigration:

Source countries	Total legal immigrants (thousands)			
	1851-60	1901-10	1981-90	1991
Total	2,598	8,795	7,629	843
Northern & Western Europe	2,407	1,874	180	32
Southern & Eastern Europe	46	6,182	356	33
Canada & Newfoundland	59	179	170	12
Latin America & Caribbean	16	183	3,613	419
Asia	57	324	2,988	306
Other or not specified	13	53	322	43

Source: Immigration and Naturalization Service Statistical Yearbook

Note: The northern and western European countries were UK, Ireland, Germany, France, Holland, Belgium, Luxembourg, Norway, Sweden, Iceland and Denmark.

Immigration problems

Each new wave of immigrants was made to feel unwelcome by those already here, even those who had arrived only a generation earlier. But our country was large, and in the 1800s there was plenty of room for new farms, new towns, and the employment of new skills in rapidly growing industries. There was enough breathing space for groups who wanted to distance themselves from others. In the cities there were conflicts over ethnic and religious differences. But even there, the "melting pot" came into operation, English rapidly becoming the common language and groups coalescing through intermarriage.

Today's immigrants face more serious problems. The United States is no longer an open and uncrowded country. The new immigrants are more racially and culturally diverse from the native population than before. Because U.S. forests are largely cut down, our water supplies and other resources becoming depleted, the pollution created by our industries and our personal life style contaminating the environment, we find it harder to absorb more people. Moreover, many industrial jobs have already been lost to company downsizing, to new technologies and to the LDCs themselves.

Nevertheless, virtually all of today's immigrants settle in our major cities, not merely because they want to, but also because they lack the means to establish and support themselves elsewhere.

Today's immigration problem differs greatly
from that of the past. The numbers involved
and the desperation are infinitely greater,
while our capacity to absorb is much smaller.

At the same time, the desperation of people to come here is more intense than ever because of their very numbers. In 1900, Europe was experiencing a natural increase (excess of births over deaths) of only about five million people a year, and the United States and other countries (Canada, Argentina, Australia, etc.) were relieving Europe of between one and two million of this growth. Today's natural increase in the LDCs is about 86 million a year. Even if these countries can send a few million people a year into Europe and North America, they are still left with an huge annual population growth which becomes increasingly difficult to absorb.

As I mentioned, there are still some Americans who feel that we should not deprive other peoples of sharing the benefits we have. We have in fact liberalized our immigration restrictions in several ways. In the late 1960s the numerical quotas that had favored northern and western Europe were replaced by new legislation which permitted much increased immigration from Asia and Africa and left intact the liberal treatment of Latin Americans. Still larger numerical limits were enacted in 1990. We had already accepted hundreds of thousands of Europeans displaced by World War II, and still later more hundreds of thousands of refugees fleeing from communist regimes. The largest number were the refugees we felt obligated to take in after the Vietnam War. We now have about one million Vietnamese, Cambodians and Laotians living in the United States today.

The great numbers of Americans who oppose our present levels of immigration do so with the conviction that:

1. Immigrants are taking jobs away from Americans, particularly from African-Americans and from immigrants already settled here.

2. Immigrants are crowding our public facilities, especially schools and hospitals, since recent immigrants have large families and high birth rates, which add greatly to the expense of state and city governments.

3. The problems in their home countries that drive them here can be solved there. Also, fertility in high-fertility countries would be reduced if people knew they couldn't leave.

There is particularly strong demand that illegal immigration be completely stopped, that illegality must not be tolerated. If we are to tolerate it, why have immigration restrictions at all? Why not declare our borders wide open to all comers?

Although illegal immigrants may pay social security and other federal taxes, do they really pay their own way, as is sometimes claimed? The major costs of their maintenance -- including birth, health care and education costs of their children -- fall on state and local governments, especially in Florida, Texas and California.

Immigrant characteristics

I do not question the fact that recent immigrants have contributed much of value to our country. Many of the legal immigrants who have arrived from Asia in recent years are highly educated. This is particularly true of immigrants from India, China and Korea, a significant proportion of whom were well educated in their home countries and also have a tradition of learning. Many of them have been very successful in their careers here. The average income of Asian Indians and Japanese here is higher even than that of white Americans. Asian-born children are often the best students in our schools. Filipino women are the mainstay of nursing staffs in many U.S. hospitals. Vietnamese refugees, despite the distress in which they fled their homeland, have made excellent adjustment to the very changed environment they found here. Whether well educated before arrival or not, Asians seem very well motivated to move up the education ladder.

Immigration

Acceptance of skilled immigrants is sometimes deplored on the ground that it is a "brain drain", that these persons are more needed in their own countries than here. Also if there are major problems in the home countries, these skilled people should be patriotic enough to stay home and help solve the problems.

Some do, of course, but their efforts are so often unrewarded. I knew very capable Indians and Sri Lankans who, either because of rigid regulation or ethnic discrimination or the very lack of resources in their countries, were unable to utilize their skills after returning home. For example, a Sri Lanka nurse who received highly specialized training in England, found on returning to Sri Lanka that only doctors were permitted to use her skills. Had she remained in England, not only would her skills have been utilized, but she would also have been able to send substantial remittances home.

But large numbers of our current immigrants are far less skilled and have a much more difficult time adapting themselves to the demands of what we consider the economy of the future. This may be particularly true of immigrants from Mexico and Central America. While we have been able to absorb many of them into our economy, because they have been willing to work hard, many problems remain.

In past periods of high immigration, no single linguistic group made up more than about 20 percent of the total immigrant numbers. Today Spanish speakers are close to half of our new arrivals. What's more, they are concentrated geographically and therefore less likely than former immigrants to coalesce with the remaining population.

Some of the newer immigrants feel resentment to their new country instead of the gratitude which earlier groups felt for the privilege of being here. Hispanics know that our southwestern states were part of Mexico before 1850; they feel they should not have had to face so many obstacles in their effort to immigrate. In addition, there are organizations that are not only very militant about Hispanic rights but which tend to encourage an attitude more of separateness than assimilation. Immigrants from Africa and the Middle East may consider our culture hostile to theirs. Muslim men, for example, may resent not being able to have multiple wives. A Palestinian friend was understandingly very resentful of our bias toward Israel, though that didn't in the least lessen his desire to immigrate. On our part, we both feel and fear immigrants' hostility, keeping in mind the 1993 bombing of the World Trade Center in New York.

Curbing illegal immigration

What can be done about illegal immigration into the United States? To patrol every mile of our long southern border would be too expensive. Some American friends living a few miles inside the border in southern Arizona tell of seeing entire families heading north on foot through their farm. Thousands of illegals are apprehended by border patrols and sent back, but only to try crossing again and this time successfully. Those who have studied the problem report that immigration from Mexico is easy and will continue so long as jobs in the United States abound, not only in agriculture but more importantly in service industries. If people cannot get into the United States on their own, there are specialists, "coyotes", who — often for a substantial fee — go back and forth between Mexican and U.S. communities and help Mexicans not only cross the border but also find jobs in places well inside the country.

Several years ago a poll taken in several Mexican communities indicated that one-third of the Mexican population wanted to come to the United States. A poll taken during 1989 in 42 Mexican communities indicated that 22 percent of those polled said that they expected to be in the United States within a year. Obviously, no such percent did immigrate in 1990. But the 22 percent figure at least, suggests the number who might come if there were no impediments.

It is also known that illegal immigrants have been able to obtain spurious documents to help them enter and stay, such as social security cards that are duplicates of cards issued to persons already here, forged "green cards" (work permits), and duplicate drivers licenses. I have already mentioned the theft of U.S. passports in Africa. In addition to the "coyotes" who bring in illegal immigrants from Mexico, there are "smugglers" who bring in Asians for large fees, which must either be paid in advance or worked off by years of virtual servitude.

Interests within our country are in conflict. There is a popular demand to restrict immigrant infiltration but there is also a labor-market interest to maintain the supply of cheap labor, manpower that is marketable since there are many jobs attractive to immigrants and less acceptable to many Americans. What some American interests perceive as a need for foreign labor is probably a mistake. There *was* a need during World War II, and the "bracero" program permitting Mexicans to come here for temporary employment satisfied that need. In most years since then, there have been plenty of Americans to meet our labor needs. We say that they don't like to do the work the Mexican immigrants do. The fact is that they won't do it for the low pay we give the Mexicans.

It must be admitted, however, that American workers are feeling the effect of immigrant competition, especially for low-pay jobs. Also, it has been noted that there has been considerable emigration of U.S. born people from states where most immigrants are settling, California, Texas, Illinois and New York. This is said to be partly due to loss of jobs to immigrants.

To tolerate illegal immigration is also unfair to the millions of foreigners who seek to come here through legal channels. There are about 3.5 million persons who have already been approved for immigration but must wait for visas until they can fall within the numerical limitations. Some have waited as long as 10 years.

Because of the great concern over illegal immigration, Congress in 1986 passed the Immigration Reform and Control Act (IRCA), to tighten up on illegal immigration and to impose fines on American employers who knowingly hire illegal immigrants. The IRCA also granted amnesty to illegal immigrants who had come before 1982. Though the IRCA has deterred illegal immigration to some extent, many believe that the pressure in Mexico is too great to hold back the tide.

That pressure stems from the inability of the Mexican economy to generate jobs for a labor force which grows rapidly as population grows. For years, U.S. firms have created plants in Mexico (known often as "maquiladoras") to take advantage of cheap labor there, and it was thought that these would give enough jobs to lessen the pressure. But some analysts point out that this has only served to acquaint Mexicans with the still better job opportunities on our side of the border and also has acquainted them — through the products they are making — with the high U.S. living standard, and therefore intensified their desire to come. Moreover, the plants where these Mexicans are employed are not in central Mexico, where population is more concentrated, but in border cities like Juarez, Nuevo Laredo, Matamoros, Mexicali and Tijuana. This has brought Mexicans closer to the windows through which they can see us and the doors through which they can enter.

Now it is believed that the North American Free Trade Agreement (NAFTA) will succeed where the maquiladoras failed. The hope is that by opening up trade, NAFTA will increase jobs and prosperity on each side of the border.

Illegal immigration can be stopped, but it may take po-lice-state tactics to stop it. A tactic already used is rounding-up a number of suspects at a workplace and summarily deporting those found to be here improperly. There is loud complaint by Mexican-American organizations and civil libertarians against all these tac-tics. Civil libertarians also oppose the proposed adoption of forge-proof social security cards or of other identification documents, which they regard as "big brother" checks.

But is stemming the illegal flow worth a police-state price?

It may become so eventually. The recent surge in immi-gration has been blamed for the increased ethnic strife in urban areas like Los Angeles and Miami, where so many new and illegal immigrants are concentrated, and where U.S. blacks face compe-tition for jobs.

Controlling entrance into our country may be far more humane in one major respect than the present lack of control. It is far less cruel to prevent people from coming in than to force them to leave once they get here. Deportation of anyone who has been here and feels that he is already "settled in," is one of the harshest experiences anyone can have.

We should remember too that the countries from which illegal immigrants come do not themselves tolerate illegal immi-gration. A Mexican consular officer once told me how tough Mexico is with illegal immigrants whom they catch. Speaking of the United States, she said, "Your immigration enforcement is a joke." Even though our civil libertarians oppose a tamper-proof ID card for U.S. citizens, Mexico has issued ID cards for its citi-zens, complete with photo and fingerprint.

Immigration

Immigration into other countries.

International migration is upon the world as never before. As I said earlier, there are an estimated 125 million people living outside the countries of their birth or citizenship. Western Europe, Canada and Australia are also having substantial immigration from developing countries. There might have been less immigration were it not that countries like Britain and Germany invited LDC workers following the close of World War II to fill perceived needs for low-paid workers. In both Germany and Britain great numbers of these workers and their families are still present, even though both countries have wished to repatriate many of them.

Australia, which for years had accepted practically no Asian immigrants, now has almost a million Asian residents, and has been second only to the United States in acceptance of Vietnamese refugees. Canada has had considerable immigration from Asia, particularly India and Hong Kong, and from Latin America. Over 20 percent of the present Canadian population and over 20 percent of the Australian are foreign-born, as opposed to only 8 percent of ours. Among the major industrial countries, only Japan has done without many foreign workers. It has, however, accepted people of Japanese ancestry from South America and also some Koreans.

For Asians, Australia is even more an immigration target than the United States. It is relatively near and has a semitropical climate. Indians see Australia as more than twice India's size with only 2 percent its population. They accuse Australia of racism for refusing to take in many millions of Indians into its "great empty spaces." Yet most of Australia is arid, and Indians who go to Australia settle only in the major cities. If you were to walk in downtown Sydney, particularly in the Kings Cross area, you would feel that persons of European blood are a minority.

The breakup of the Soviet Union and the former Yugoslavia and other changes in eastern Europe, have resulted in large-scale migration, particularly of refugees into Germany, which until 1993 was accepting all those seeking asylum. The refugee flows elsewhere in the world, such as Africa, where millions of people are already displaced from their homes, are very likely to increase. Also, despite what has seemed a peaceful transition in South Africa, many thousands of whites may want to leave for predominantly white countries.

Refugees

Coming as a refugee or an asylum seeker is now the method of choice for getting past barriers into the United States or various European countries — and bringing one's children. We all know that illegal immigration is illegal, and the question is what can be done to stop it. Refugees, on the other hand, may be entering with a considerable degree of legality.

Refugees are those people who are fleeing or have fled from their homelands, and who are claiming to be in fear of the persecution or physical harm they would suffer if they returned or remained there. There are millions of such people throughout the world. In 1994 there may be as many as 20 million people displaced from their homelands for such fears, and another 15 million internally displaced within their homelands. At least half the displacements are in Africa, with Rwandans the most recent example.

Some of the African refugees included in the above numbers are persons displaced primarily because of famine, or a combination of famine and persecution. In times of famine, it is obvious that disfavored or persecuted ethnic groups are the ones most likely to suffer hunger.

In the past, people fleeing from persecution in their homelands were often individual dissidents, or were members of minority groups constituting small percentages of the homeland population. The Jews who lived in Germany when Hitler came to power were only one percent of the German population. Many of the Jews who died in the Holocaust could have been saved if they had been accepted in other countries as refugees before World War II began.

Memory of the Holocaust prompted the adoption of U.N. protocols calling on nations to offer refuge to persons fleeing their homelands with a well-founded fear of persecution for political, racial or religious reasons. But it was hardly expected that the protocols would have to cover the large-scale population movements of today.

Immigration

Refugees who are already in a country where they hope to remain are sometimes called "asylees," meaning persons who are seeking asylum in that country. During Cold War days, people asked asylum as defectors from communist countries; they had come legally on visitor or diplomatic visas, but then sought to stay because they claimed it was unsafe to return to their country of origin or because they felt it oppressive to have to live under communist rule. Usually we welcomed them, less for humanitarian reasons than as a way to discredit communism. We also accepted many Soviet Jews, and criticized the Soviet Union for not granting Jews more exit visas.

Refugee legislation

The United States has often, either by Congressional or executive action, admitted several classes of refugees over and above immigration quotas. Under 1946 legislation, hundreds of thousands of displaced persons from central and eastern Europe were admitted. In later years, we admitted groups of refugees from many other countries, including Hungary, Cuba, Haiti and Ethiopia. The largest group of refugees we have admitted have been 900,000 Indo-Chinese (from Vietnam, Laos and Cambodia). Their admission began in 1975 and continued over a period of years.

Even though the United States has accepted more refugees for permanent settlement than all other countries in the world combined, we are still strongly criticized for not accepting more. We are also criticized for the fact that most of the refugees we have admitted have been those fleeing from communist countries, such as Cuba, Vietnam and the Soviet Union. At the same time we rejected people coming illegally from El Salvador or those seeking to come by boat from Haiti, on the grounds that they were coming for economic betterment, just as those who enter illegally from Mexico. Though we did admit some Haitian refugees under 1980 refugee legislation, not to mention many thousand more who were admitted as legal immigrants (47,000 in 1991 alone), we have turned back thousands of others who have sought to come here by boat.

Refugees from what — from communism?

As already mentioned, we actually encouraged any visitors from the Soviet Union to "defect" and remain here, as if to show the world by their presence here how much better our country was than theirs. On a few occasions we have even used pressure to keep some of them here.

The 1980 Refugee Act recognized the existence of refugees as persons who have a well-founded fear of persecution in their own countries, but it was not an open door to admit all such persons, nor could it have been, because the numbers involved are so large. The Act leaves it to our government's discretion as to which refugees and how many should be admitted. The selection has always been in favor of persons from communist countries.

We were unduly generous to Cuban refugees. Because the Castro regime is communist and Castro was an ally of the Soviets, we have not only treated Cuba as an enemy country and embargoed it, but we also welcomed Cubans here as refugees from communism and admitted them in large numbers. Close to a million Cubans have been admitted since Castro came to power in 1959, including 125,000 who came during 1980 in what was called the Mariel boatlift.

Our preference for Cubans over Haitians was unjustified. The sufferings of Cuban people under Castro do not compare with the torture, murder and rape of Haitian people by the Duvaliers and by the military regime which followed them. Even though we may not admit it, Castro brought Cuba many social benefits, including better health care and education than any other Latin Americans have enjoyed. Naturally, Cubans dislike Castro's authoritarian regime, and thousands also want to join relatives in Florida.

The Cuban economic situation of recent years, worsened by our embargo and the phasing out of Soviet help, has made life miserable for the typical Cuban. But to a large extent, Cubans have the same motives for coming to the United States as millions of other Latin Americans. That is why so many headed here on boats when Castro eased their emigration in August 1994, in effect permitting another Mariel. The Clinton administration's response was to equate the treatment of Cuban and Haitian boat people and to provide safe haven in Guantanamo and elsewhere for both groups, rather than admission to our mainland as political refugees.

Or refugees from the results of our own misdoings?

Let's face it. It was the Vietnam War, and the plight of our South Vietnamese allies when the war ended, that obligated us to admit hundreds of thousands of Indo-Chinese refugees. Even had we won the war, the links we formed with the Indo-Chinese would have resulted in large numbers coming here, just as our historical links with the Filipinos have resulted in so many of them being here. We have not taken in corresponding numbers of Thais, Malaysians or Indonesians, since we had no such links with them.

We didn't want the refugees from El Salvador to come here, but over half a million managed to come here anyway. One reason for their coming was that we armed and funded the "death squads" in that country who killed not only tens of thousands of peasants but also many intellectuals and church people. The death squads weren't the only reason, but they certainly did their part. Just as there needn't have been a Vietnam War, there needn't have been the kind of involvement we had in Central America in support of the Nicaraguan "contras" and the El Salvador death squads.

And even a part of Haiti's troubles may be attributed to our misdoings with respect to that country. Our marines occupied it for 19 years. Later, when "Papa Doc" Duvalier took over, we were unnecessarily supportive of his regime and his son's.

Or refugees from overpopulation?

However, El Salvador is a very overcrowded country — the most densely populated mainland country in the Americas. Even before its civil war, Salvadorans were fleeing first into less crowded neighbor Honduras, then into Mexico and then here after both Honduras and Mexico refused to settle any more people. Some who have written about the country's plight blame overpopulation for the conditions which led to its civil war. El Salvador has never had a particularly benign government, but neither has its neighbor Honduras. Yet relatively few people have fled from Honduras. Honduras has a low enough population density that it has a modest degree of land ownership among its peasants.

Observers have said of El Salvador that it will never have real land reform because there's not enough land to reform.

Can it not be said that even though many of the Salvadorans who fled here fled for their lives, they were overpopulation refugees as much as they were political refugees? Now that peace has returned to El Salvador at least in the election process, do we see many of the Salvadorans here wanting to return home?

A somewhat similar case can be made about Haitians. Haiti has had oppressive rule for many decades. But Haiti has the highest total fertility rate and lowest contraceptive use of any country in the Americas. Even before Haitians came by boat in large numbers to Florida, Haitians were overflowing into the Dominican Republic and also into the Bahamas, which finally took action to keep them back.

Nobody in our government, and for that matter almost nobody in public life, has been willing even to suggest that there is a population-environment factor in Haitian troubles. But the international explorer Jacques-Yves Cousteau described Haiti as one of the most disaster-ravaged spots on earth. In an address to the UN Conference on Environment and Development, he said:

"Haiti is terribly overpopulated: 7.5 million people on an exiguous and impoverished land. Six children per family, but fathers of eleven are not rare. High infant death rate, insufficient schooling, and misery due to ignorance, superstition and poor political management. [Haitians] have exhausted the marine resources of their narrow continental shelf. They have deforested two-thirds of their country to cook their meals, they continue to deforest, and turn wood into charcoal. We asked: 'What will you do when there is no wood left at all?' 'That will be the end of the world!' they replied. Until then, the men of Haiti procreate, hoping that their male children will take care of their old fathers; and the women say, 'I am not the one to decide how many children I will have.' "

This may explain why the proportion of women using birth control is lower in Haiti than anywhere else in the Caribbean. Contraception is not new to Haiti, however, and surveys have shown that the majority of Haitian women know about it. They simply don't use it.

Immigration

Haitians have been landing in Florida by boat since the early 1970s. So many others have managed to come here, whether legally or illegally, that their number in the United States is believed to be almost a million. Perhaps as many live in the New York area as in Florida.

The Cuban and Haitian crises

As you know, the Clinton administration faced major and acute political crises during 1994 with respect to Cuba and Haiti. The Cuban crisis necessitated negotiations with Cuba, which prior administrations had shunned in their aversion to dealing with Cuba as a communist enemy. President Clinton was roundly criticized for the concessions made to the Castro regime. The Haitian crisis brought even stronger criticism, since it necessitated military occupation of Haiti.

What was most at stake in both these crises was protection of our borders from floods of immigrants claiming refugee status. Without this threat and without the insistence by refugee advocates and U.S. black leaders that we give Haitians sanctuary, it is doubtful that we would have taken action on Haiti.

Closely related to the immigration issue is the population issue. This is less true in Cuba's case than in Haiti's, since Cuban fertility is low and Cuba's environment has been less devastated than Haiti's. But Haiti's situation is so desperate that great numbers of Haitians will continue to seek immigration here. And since almost nobody, American or Haitian, will admit the enormity of the population problem, no early population solution is likely.

The worldwide search for asylum

I called the Haitian and Cuban crises acute. The chronic problem, which the United States shares with Canada and several other developed countries, notably Germany, is that the claim of political asylum has become an abused tool for circumventing immigration restrictions. It is used by immigration seekers as if it were a form of permanent immigration. The United States now receives over 100,000 new political asylum claims a year, far more than our adjudication machinery can handle. The backlog of unresolved claims now exceeds 400,000. The resources that would be needed to process all these claims would better be used to improve conditions in the claimants' home countries.

World Population Growth

Germany's situation was even more troubling, for Germany has had hundreds of thousands of refugees from Bosnia and Croatia begging admission, as well as many thousands from Asia and Africa. Because Germany wants to disclaim completely its Nazi past, it admitted over half a million people in 1992 for asylum.

But in 1993, Germany took steps to slow down the admission of asylum seekers. This has angered not only outsiders but Germans as well. But we might well ask, "Is it fair for a country of 80 million people, already overcrowded and burdened with the problems of integrating former East Germans into its labor force, to be sharply criticized for not accepting all comers from the outside?"

And what of us? We are finding that the processing of asylum claims has become extremely costly as compared to the processing of immigration applications through the regular consular channels. Thousands of people arrive every month at our international airports, demanding political asylum instead of showing travel visas. Even undocumented Mexicans are claiming political asylum when they are apprehended and face possible deportation. People smuggled onto our shores from China are claiming — and receiving — asylum, on the ground that they are victims of China's family-size limits. If we are trying to limit our own fertility, these are certainly the very people we don't want in our country.

And what do we do while asylum claims are pending? Do we intern asylum claimants into detention centers, as Hong Kong has done, and as we ourselves have used Guantanamo? If we release claimants into our population at large, how do we know that they will ever show up months later for their claims to be heard. Unlike Germany, which has long had effective systems of police checks, ours is an open society in which foreigners can easily "get lost."

Moreover, refugee and asylum status should be treated as permission for temporary stay only, not as permanent immigration. A system to insure that the stay is only temporary should be humane, but it also must be effective. Refugees and asylees should be admitted only if they agree that they will return to their homelands when conditions are safe, and that meanwhile they keep their whereabouts known to authorities at all times.

Immigration

It is time for an international review of the refugee-asylee situation to stop abuses and bring the numbers of claims under control. The High Commission for Refugees might be able to enumerate the most urgent cases and recommend acceptance quotas to individual countries. It should not be left up to the individual refugee to decide which country should accept him.

Some further thoughts

There are no simple solutions to the problems we and other advanced countries face in the matter of immigration and refugee admission. But here are some thoughts which I'd like to pass along to you.

First, there are great problems in many countries which drive people to seek admission here as immigrants and refugees. Some are very tragic political problems such as those of Bosnia; these can hardly claim be described as primarily population problems. But most problems in the developing countries, whether they involve political oppression, tribal conflict or famine, are population problems primarily or even wholly. If populations in these countries were smaller, and if competing groups had more breathing space between them, these problems would certainly be of less impact.

Second, there are very few places of possible refuge left in the world. *This of itself is a population problem.* The few large places left are inhospitable areas like the Sahara Desert, the Australian deserts, and the northern expanses of Siberia and Canada. In the 19th century and in the early 20th, there were livable, uncrowded places to which people could migrate, in the Americas, in Africa, and in the Russian empire.

But these places are no longer uncrowded; people seeking to move into them would find great resistance from people already there. In 1903, the British colony of Uganda was suggested as a possible sanctuary for European Jews. Even though it straddled the equator, it was high enough to have a temperate climate, and it was then sparsely populated. Today Uganda is so crowded and has had so much unrest that many of its 20 million people are desperate to leave.

Third, whenever possible we should first seek solutions within the home countries themselves. Eventually, a population solution must be found for Haiti, and for other countries as well. We should be prepared to tell people in these countries, "Your overpopulation is of your own making. We will assist you with your developmental needs and with stopping population growth itself. But your population problem is a responsibility you must accept; don't try to get out of it by sending us your excess people."

Because many of those seeking immigration to the United States are dark-skinned, we are charged with racism toward any we do not accept. Such a charge will be made regardless of what we do. Our rejection of people as immigrants does not at all mean that we hate them or regard them as inferior to ourselves. *Our problem with the people seeking to come is not with their color but with their numbers.* We must emphasize that there is a carrying capacity beyond which we find it most difficult to accept immigrants or refugees. Their own countries have immigration limits too, and in all likelihood they enforce those limits more rigorously than we enforce ours.

Even then, there are situations where we will have to exercise both compassion and oversight rather than our better judgment. People in some of these troubled countries are so desperate that there is nothing we can do other than to continue taking some of them in. And for the time being, we will find it very difficult to keep them out. But ultimately, we and the more affluent countries like ours will have to insist on firm limits. For if we in America accept too many immigrants and refugees, the America they had been seeking will be lost to them as well as to us.

Do You Want to Come to the United States?

If so, you're one of many millions. The 260 million people now in the USA include recent newcomers from every country of the world, of all races, all religions, all languages. Each year the number legally admitted for permanent residence here may exceed the number admitted to all other countries combined.

All over the world, there are great numbers of people whose greatest hope in life is to come here. This is because, despite its problems, our country tries to provide well for all its people. To be admitted here is a valued privilege, and most people who live here are deeply grateful for it.

But don't feel angry at us if you haven't been admitted. During this past year over a million people were welcomed to live here permanently, including a large number from your country. But each million will be only a small fraction of the many millions who apply for admission.

We limit the numbers we welcome to this country to protect the welfare of those who have already come. To admit too many people would cause more unemployment, more overcrowding, and more difficulty in providing needed services such as education, health care, housing, water, electricity, sanitation and security. All countries restrict immigration for these reasons.

If we were to take in all the millions who wish to come, we would be so overpopulated in relation to resources that newcomers might find conditions here worse than those they left behind.

We ask you not to try to enter our country illegally. You would not want anyone to enter your home without your permission, and this is the way we feel about those who come here without our consent. Millions of people have been approved for legal entry and are awaiting their turn to come. For others to try to cut in ahead of them would be unfair. Most Americans welcome legal immigrants, but the concern over illegal entry tends to prejudice many people against all immigration.

One reason for the worsening conditions in many countries is rapid population growth. World population will have quadrupled in this century, growing from about 1.5 billion to 6.0 billion. In your country too, the population may have more than tripled. Death rates have decreased so rapidly that families no longer need to have more than two children. Limiting future births will greatly help the welfare of children already born, and you can help your country's efforts to slow its population growth.

137

World Population Growth

Even though our country has only two children per family, we have been justly criticized for having too wasteful a life style, consuming far too much of the earth's resources and causing too much pollution. We may be compelled to lead simpler lives in future years. People coming here in the hope that they will have a luxurious life style may be disappointed.

Do You Want to Come to the United States?

¿Quiere usted venir a los Estados Unidos?

Si es así, usted es uno de muchos millones de personas que o desean. Entre los 260 millones de personas que ahora viven en EE.UU. se encuentran los recién llegados de todos los países del mundo, gente de todas las razas, religiones y lenguas. Más de un millón de personas son admitidas legalmente cada año como residentes en este país, una cifra que es probablemente superior a la todos los demás países juntos. Entre ellos se encuentra un grupo numeroso de personas de su propio país. Vivir aquí es un privilegio que valora y aprecia profundamente la mayoría de las personas que lo disfrutan.

No se enoje con nosotros si no le han dado entrada todavía. El millón de personas que entran anualmente es solamente una fracción de los muchos millones que solicitan admisión. Se impone esta limitación con el fin de proteger el bienestar de aquellos que ya están aquí. Si se permite entrada a un número demasiado grande de personas habría más desempleo y hacinamiento, y sería más difícil suministrar los servicios necesarios como educación, cuidado sanitario, vivienda, agua, electricidad, servicios higiénicos y de protección. Las mismas razones por las que otros países restringen la inmigración. Todos los países de latinoamérica, incluyendo el suyo, son mucho más restrictivos que nosotros en cuanto a la recepción de inmigrantes.

Si nosotros diéramos entrada a todos esos millones de personas que desean hacerlo, nuestra población excedería tanto nuestros recursos que los recién llegados se encontrarían con unas condiciones peores que las que dejaron atrás. El sueño anhelado ya no existiría.

Existen mecanismos legales para poder solicitar admisión al país; por lo tanto, les rogamos que no traten de hacerlo de manera ilegal. A usted no le gustaría que alguien entrara a su hogar sin su permiso; nosotros también pensamos igual de los que vienen a este país sin nuestro consentimiento. Hay millones de personas aprobadas para ingresar legalmente y están esperando su turno de entrada. Sería injusto que otros se les adelantaran. La mayoría de la gente en Estados Unidos tiene una actitud acogedora hacia los inmigrantes, muchos propenden a tener una opinión adversa contra todo tipo de inmigración y de inmigrantes por los que entran de manera ilegal.

World Population Growth

El rápido crecimiento demográfico en muchos países ha causado un deterioro en sus condiciones de vida. Al finalizar el siglo la población mundial se habrá cuadruplicado, aumentando de 1.9 millones a 6 mil millones. También en su país la población ha crecido rápidamente debido al crecimiento de la familia. La tasa de mortalidad ha disminuido tanto que ya no es necesario tener más de dos niños por familia. La limitación de la natalidad ayudaría enormemente a mejorar el bienestar de los niños ya nacidos, y usted puede ayudar a que su país reduzca la tasa de natalidad.

A pesar que en nuestro país hay solamente un promedio de dos niños por familia, nuestro propio crecimiento nos obligaría a adoptar estilos de vida mucho más sencillos que en los años anteriores. Quienes vienen aquí con la esperanza de tener un estilo de vida luminoso podrían sufrir una desilución.

Do You Want to Come to the United States?

你想来美国吗?

如果是的话, 你与成千万的其它人一样.

目前居住在美国的二亿六千万人包括来自全世界各国家, 各个种族, 各种宗教, 以及各种语言的新近移民. 每一年, 合法进入美国成为永久居民的人次 超过一百万人. 这个数字大概超过全世界各个国家接纳移民的总数. 能够获得居留 许可是一种特权 大多数享有此项特权的人也都极为珍惜这项权利.

假如你还没有获得入境许可, 请不要对我们生气. 我们所接纳的每一百万人仅是其它正在申请居留人数的一小部分而已. 我们限制入境人数是为了保障那些已经来的人的福利. 如果我们接收太多移民会导致更高的失业率, 更拥挤的状况, 同时也会加重提供如教育, 医疗保健, 住房, 水, 电, 卫生, 安全等服务的负担 在对移民的接纳程度上, 大多数的其它国家, 可能也包括您的国家 要比我们来得低.

如果我们敞开大门接受所有想进入美国的人, 那么我们将面临人口膨胀的问题, 同时有限的资源也会被耗尽. 如此一来, 新来者将发现美国的情况比母国更糟. 他们所追求的美国将不再存在.

我们希望您不要试图非法入境美国. 您大概也不希望别人没有您的允许不要进入您的国家. 我们对非法移民也持相同的看法.

不按正当程序插队而进入美国的人对于好几百万已经获得美国政府入境许可而正在苦苦地排队等候名额的人而言是不公平的. 大多数的美国人欢迎合法移民, 但是对非法移民的关切已使得许多美国人对所有的移民问题以及所有的移民产生偏见.

我们对于中国与其它国家的家庭人口数量大小也有同样的关切. 人口膨胀是一个严重的问题. 在我们这个时代, 鼓励夫妻养育一或二个儿女应该是一项正确的做法. 如果您来美国的目的是为了生育更多的子女, 那我们希望您不要来.

或者, 假如您来美国是为了过舒适, 豪华的生活, 您可能会很失望 这是因为大多数的国家都面临资源短缺的问题. 即便是我们美国人也必须过着比过去更为简朴的生活.

Translated by Yih-Jin Young

141

Chapter 16

The Roman Catholic Position

"The cry for birth control led eventually to ...
abortion on demand."
— Judie Brown, President of the American Life League

The opposition of the Roman Catholic Church to all forms of birth control, other than "natural family planning," or the "rhythm method," is universally known. What you may not know is that even the rhythm method was not intended for general use. According to the 1930 encyclical of Pope Pius XI, it is to be availed of only in situations of temporary emergency such as acute poverty. Sexual intercourse has traditionally been regarded by the Catholic Church as a privilege granted by God to enable man to "be fruitful and multiply." The 1968 encyclical of Paul VI, "Humanae Vitae," made it clear that every sex act must be open to the transmission of human life.

However, it is interesting to note that the Catholic Church has never ruled that sexual intercourse is sinful in cases of a woman's involuntary sterility, such as during pregnancy or after menopause.

Doctrine vs. practice

Can we say that the Church's prohibition of artificial birth control is responsible for most of the excess population growth throughout the world, particularly in Latin America? Is it to be blamed for most of the misery associated with high birth rates and overpopulation? The answer is mostly, but not entirely: No.

World Population Growth

For one thing, the regions of the world where birth rates are highest, Africa and the Middle East, have very few Roman Catholics. In Europe and North America, Catholics have no higher birth rates than non-Catholics, so that one would wonder how much influence the Church has over its own members. In Europe, the country with nearly the lowest birth rate is Italy, with Vatican City in its very midst, and where the majority of people are nominally Catholic. Spain, another Catholic country, also has a very low birth rate. In the United States, four of the five states with the largest proportions of Catholics, Massachusetts, Rhode Island, Connecticut and New Jersey, have almost the lowest birth rates in the country. Utah, the state with the lowest proportion of Catholics, has the highest birth rate. In Canada, although largely Catholic Quebec once was the province with the highest birth rate, it now has the lowest.

For many years, Roman Catholics in the United States were found to have larger families than non-Catholics, but this is no longer the case. Catholic women practice contraception as much as non-Catholic and may possibly have as many abortions. It is said that Catholic women resort to sterilization even more than non-Catholic. The facetious explanation is that sterilization would require only one confession, whereas using the contraceptive pill would require daily confession.

In most Asian countries, Catholics, or for that matter, Christians, are definitely in the minority. Yet in most of these countries, Christian, including Catholics, have definitely more contraceptive use and lower fertility than their non-Christian neighbors. This may be partly due to the fact that the urban and the more educated parts of the population have been drawn to Christianity. Fertility is high in the Philippines, a predominantly Catholic country. But again Muslim fertility there is distinctly higher than Catholic.

So now let's turn to Latin America. My own observations there are limited. I have worked only in Guatemala and Colombia, and in total only a few months. I could see, particularly in the latter country, that only women pay much attention to Church teachings; most men tend to ignore them. But in the past at least, many Latin American men prided themselves on large families. When men have insisted on having many children, women usually complied.

The Roman Catholic Position

As I mentioned earlier, the Church in Mexico is said to have perceived the country's population problem even before the government did. In Colombia, I found that priests had considerable compassion for the plight of women and their too frequent pregnancies. They were alarmed by the all too common abortions, and openly said that contraception of some sort was needed to prevent them.

But Catholic conservatives here at home, such as Judie Brown of the American Life League, claim that it was the legalization and widespread use of contraception that led to the demand for abortion. They also reason that easily available contraception has encouraged sexual license among the unmarried. They point out that, despite all the public money spent for birth control, out-of-wedlock births have increased to over a million a year.

But what about the millions of married women who are spared by modern contraception from the many unwanted pregnancies that women years ago had to endure? Does the Church want to roll back this change? Does the Church take the position that children are God's punishment of their parents for having had sex?

The political arena

Even though the Church's teachings on birth control are not adhered to by its members, the Church has tremendous political influence in the United States. It has joined with the so-called "religious right" in opposition not only to abortion, but also to the funding of family planning, either at home or in the LDCs. There is no question that legislators, whether Catholic or not, give close heed to the Church's position.

I have had several conversations with Catholic conservatives, including spokespersons for the Seattle Archdiocese. They have reminded me that the Church has recognized the relation of population growth to poverty in developing countries. They have quoted Papal statements to the effect that these problems can be solved by measures other than birth control, such as generous financial assistance and large-scale international migration. Archdiocese representatives have told me that U.S. restrictions against Latin American immigration are inhuman and should be lifted.

World Population Growth

The Vatican took a very strong position against abortion at the Conference in Cairo. Keep in mind, however, that the Conference did not at all promote abortion. Instead, it took the position that contraception should be freely available in order to prevent abortion. Has the Vatican ever thought of the millions of abortions which have taken place in Catholic countries, and which would not have taken place except for the Church's ban on contraception?

Many Catholic women have begun to question whether the Church speaks for them. They note that the Church is a male-ruled body, in which women are not even allowed to serve as priests. Unmarried women who serve as nuns are not representative of Catholic women generally. Two organizations of Catholic lay people, Catholics Speak Out and Catholics for a Free Choice, have challenged Church positions on contraception and abortion.

On the suffering of women due to unwanted pregnancies, the conservatives have offered no response. Perhaps they would simply say, like some pro-life demonstrators, "If she didn't want a baby, she shouldn't have had sex." But sadly enough it is in Catholic countries such as in Latin America that women have been taught that they must never refuse their husbands' demands for sex.

The Catholic Church is outstanding in its humane concern in so many areas of world affairs and particularly in its quest for economic justice and the amelioration of the exploitive tendencies of capitalism. I wish it had more compassion for those women who have no way other than birth control to protect themselves from the burden of excessive pregnancies imposed on them by men. And I also wish it had more concern for the disadvantaged children who will be born from these pregnancies.

The Roman Catholic Position

The future

Will official Catholic doctrine on birth control ever change?

Probably, at least to the extent of approving contraception if not abortion. It will of course be difficult for any Pope to admit that his predecessors were wrong. But the Church may become so concerned about population and other social problems that pro-responsible parenthood will become a more important doctrinal issue than anti-birth control. Some observers felt that Pope John XXIII was considering doctrinal change before his death, since he commissioned a study to review the Church's position. A prominent observer also believes that John Paul I might have challenged the position had he survived beyond his one-month tenure.

Chapter 17

Compulsion vs. Education

"Informed free choice is essential to the long-term success of family planning programmes."
— The Cairo conference document

Nobody likes compulsion. Whatever you think about abortion, I hope you agree with me that no woman should be compelled to bear a child against her will, or more children than she wants to bear.

But what about trying to prevent women from bearing more than two children — or to prevent them from bearing more than one, as China did, and still tries to do, in the large cities? Women throughout the world are seeking reproductive freedom. For many of them that means freedom for any woman to bear as many children as she wants. Is that the freedom women must enjoy?

Some would say "No". Prof. Garrett Hardin of the University of California, Santa Barbara, has written, "Freedom to breed is intolerable," that an individual's freedom must yield to the higher interests of society.

Must individual fertility decisions
yield to the interests of society?

Most of you would probably say that the way to deal with the population problem is: Educate instead of compel. And how long must we continue to educate instead of compel? Until the

149

U.S. population reaches 500 million or the world population reaches 12 billion? Wouldn't it be wiser to consider some compulsion measures before that?

Compulsion versus incentives

We have already described China's one-child policy, and the fact that the Chinese government has had to relax it except in the cities. We can still say that the policy is very close to direct compulsion. And yet we can understand the reasons for its adoption, and also note that the policy has been fairly effective.

India's policy during the 1970s was more of the nature of incentives and disincentives. But in 1975-77, it too proved to be too coercive and had to be relaxed. But there is no question that India's population today is lower than it would have been without the millions of vasectomies which were performed in 1975-77.

Singapore was highly successful in its incentive-disincentive program. It gave valuable awards to families who had only one or two children, including much better schooling for those children, much better housing for the families. There was almost no protest against the program. Fertility fell to replacement level very quickly. But Singapore was a sophisticated urban community where good education and good housing were greatly valued, so the program worked. Perhaps Singapore's fertility would have rapidly dropped even without the program.

Other political abuses in India contributed to Indira Gandhi's downfall, not the vasectomy campaign alone. In China, the government might have had more willing acceptance of its family limitation policy had it been democratic in other respects — no persecution of dissidents, no Tiananmen Square massacres.

Critics have even disparaged Singapore's highly successful incentive-disincentive program. As the children of parents who had large families were denied the same educational advantages as children in small families, the critics claim that such children were unduly penalized. After all, why penalize the children for a choice their parents made? Singapore's authoritarian government has been criticized for many things — for its use of corporal punishment, for example — and the criticism of its population policy was part of the broader criticism.

Incentives and disincentives do indeed contain elements of compulsion. The Cairo Document itself urged against them, saying that efforts should focus on "voluntary measures rather than schemes involving incentives and disincentives."

Another serious problem with incentives is that people accept treatments that they may not want but can't afford to turn down. If the incentive offered to accept a sterilization or an IUD is equivalent to a number of months' income, how can a poor person refuse it? Women have been paid to accept IUDs even when the doctors or paramedics who inserted the IUD should have known that the IUD was likely to cause not only constant pain but also serious infection.

In an earlier chapter, I discussed the complaints of women leaders that family-planning programs are too male-managed, too impersonal, too numerically measured, and that they involve too much regimentation of women. An even stronger complaint is that the programs were introduced by foreigners rather than by natives.

Though I acknowledge the validity of these complaints, I nevertheless feel that in the two countries where I worked in this very numerical measurement, Sri Lanka and India, the benefit from the fertility reductions which have taken place far outweighed the regimentation costs. I do wish that the family-planning efforts had been initiated and effectively pursued by nationals, so that outsiders like myself had never become involved in it. But I do not like to think of how much worse the present situation of these countries would have been without these fertility reductions.

Other forms of compulsion or incentives

A woman who worked with me in India offered to help an individual family with several children provided they would agree not to have additional children. She felt that the family would be tempted to have more children if they saw that money was coming in regularly. So what she did was to promise to send the family some amount like $50 each month, with the stipulation that if an additional child was born, the money would stop. Of course, she might instead have stipulated that one of the parents have a sterilization first, and then she wouldn't need to follow up on what births there might be after she went back home.

World Population Growth

The various U.S. organizations who assign a child from a poor LDC family for you to "adopt" by sending $10 or so a month, would almost certainly refuse to approve any such stipulation, probably calling it a form of compulsion. Some of the organizations are Catholic and would view the stipulation as promoting birth control. And yet I can appreciate the wisdom of my former fellow-worker.

But what about incentives/disincentives at an international level? Should the United Nations, or the United States, or any other country, cut off economic aid or declare sanctions if a country hasn't taken reasonable steps to reduce its people's fertility? Should the United States impose tougher immigration restrictions on a high-fertility country, or ban all immigration from that country until its fertility falls to replacement level? Proposals just like these have sometimes been made.

Philip Hauser of the University of Chicago once wrote that no sane statesmen would even consider such a position. He perhaps was right at that time, for we were competing with the Soviet Union for the Third World's favor.

But I have asked myself what might have been the result if during the 1960s we would have made our massive food aid to India contingent on firm family planning measures, like the very measures that India adopted during 1975-77. To me it is quite conceivable that India's population today would be far less than it now is. Knowing Somalia's high fertility rate and its cultural rejection of family planning, we might have said to the Somalis: We're feeding you this time, but only on condition that you immediately adopt a vigorous fertility-reduction policy. If your fertility rate is not 30 percent lower at your next famine, we will refuse to help you.

*Can our views be imposed on
another nation, even if it's
for their own good?*

Garrett Hardin, whom I quoted earlier in this chapter, is a great exponent of "tough love." This is the harsh discipline that some parents inflict upon a child whom they deeply love, because they know, or at least believe, that this will benefit the child in the

Compulsion vs. Education

long run. Hardin also writes of "lifeboat ethics," describing a situation where a lifeboat cannot take from the water even one additional drowning person without sinking itself. If someone already in the lifeboat greatly desires to save an additional person, he should give up his own place to that person rather than endanger others in the boat.

It is with views like these that Hardin approaches such issues as famine relief, immigration, etc. He says that each nation is responsible for itself. He rejects the ideas that we are all one world and that we will necessarily suffer if we ignore the sufferings of others. He would probably say that Somalia will now have increased fertility because of our having fed them. He may be right.

But I would reject his stern views, at least for the present, and would hope that the policies outlined in the Cairo Conference program of action — backed up by a great amount of education and persuasion — will result in achieving the Conference goals. The education and persuasion I would urge would include the teaching I stress in this book, namely, persuading parents that love for their own children will lead them not to have more than two. And particularly educating and persuading today's children, who will be the next generation of parents.

But it is possible that the time may come — if these goals are not met during the next few decades — when international policy makers may adopt the compulsion that we now seek to avoid.

Chapter 18

Do We Love Our Children?

"Unto us a child is born ... and
  his name shall be called Wonderful"
— Isaiah (9:6)

The United Nations World Summit for Children, held in New York in September 1990, was the occasion for many important statements by world leaders and others on the great need for the love and care of the world's children. The following statement by Chile's President, Patricio Aylwin, was typical of the sentiments expressed: "Our love for our children should be on our minds 24 hours a day."

At the Summit, many Third World delegates also described the specific perils threatening children in their own countries — health hazards, famine, poverty, illiteracy, civil war. But I did not read any mention of overpopulation, oversized families, or the consequences of these situations.

In this chapter, I am urging that both the billions of people in the developing countries and the millions of people in our own country show their love for children by bearing fewer of them, and by refraining from bearing children for whom they can't provide. But I am also urging that we do infinitely more than we are doing to relieve the poverty of billions of children already here on earth, including poverty in our own country. This work will require great quantities of money, with the bulk of that money going for the benefit of children in the LDCs, since they are the ones most in need. Much of the money would have to come from us

155

Americans. But I am also hoping that Americans will also spend more money for our own American children.

The U.N. Declaration of the Rights of the Child enumerates several rights, including rights to nutrition, to education, etc. One of the rights is the right to love and affection. Shouldn't this right include the *right not to be born* until the child's parents are able and ready to provide for him?

People in India and Sri Lanka used to tell me how much they loved their children. I am sure that their children were much valued, though in Indian families boys were much more valued than girls. It was very important for married couples to have children. For a woman in India, not to have a son was a mark of shame. In West Africa also, for a woman to be childless was a matter of great concern. Having children before marriage was often a valued experience, proving that the woman was fecund. American women who worked in villages in the Peace Corps, for example, were often pitied by villagers for not having children.

People from the LDCs who visit Europe or North America express surprise at how few children are on the streets, even in suburban and rural areas, as compared to the large numbers typically seen every day in their own homelands. They often ask whether we of the western world have only a few children because we don't love or value them.

But much of the desire for children — or at least, for large families — may be associated with the parents' perceived economic need, as described by Mamdani in "The Myth of Population Control." Or it may be tied in with the need to perpetuate one's family name or to enhance the prestige of the husband and of his clan or extended kinship. To the extent that this is the case, one may distinguish this desire — intense as it may be — from pure or selfless love.

When one realizes that many of the children born as the result of this type of desire may have more difficulty in life than would children born into small families and into a society of small families, one may question just what the parental love is.

It's the same for the children who are born merely as the result of sexual desire. The American unwed mother who has engaged in sex recklessly and without regard for the birth consequences may not love her child as genuinely, even though she may claim to, as the woman who waits for a stable marriage to a loving husband. In past decades, young women may have hoped to snare a husband by getting pregnant. But today the unwed mother has a much poorer chance of getting married than an unencumbered woman. By getting pregnant and having a child, she has hurt herself as well as her child.

Isabel Sawhill of the Urban Institute, recognizing the claim that a woman may react to the lack of marriageable males by having a child out of wedlock, writes as follows:

"Why doesn't she postpone childbearing until she herself is better prepared to meet the responsibility? In the meantime, she might also become a more attractive marriage mate. If the problem is 'too few men' to go around, women might be expected to compete for those who are available by not tying themselves down with young children."

Elsewhere, she also describes what most Americans have always considered to be a proper societal norm:

"No one is expected to parent a child before they have the personal and financial resources to support that child ... until one has completed one's schooling and at least one parent has secured regular employment."

The woman, whether wed or unwed, who is addicted to drugs, to cigarettes, to alcohol, or who has a disease (such as AIDS) which might be transmitted, and who yet allows herself to become pregnant and then bear a child — does she really love that child, knowing, as she certainly does, that the child might suffer from her disease or addiction?

We sometimes read of the woman whose life is so empty that she feels she needs a baby who will be someone she can love and will love her. Or of the mother who says that having a baby inside her is the only time she feels she is alive.

Much as we can understand these feelings, we can still ask: Is it really love, love to a child, when we bear the child into a setting where we know he will start out his life in deep handicap?

Can we distinguish between having a child for one's own sake and having a child for the child's sake? Mamdani's Indian villagers, if he quotes them correctly, are having children primarily for their own sake, because their own living standard will be enhanced — or they think it will be enhanced — because of their many children. But unless they weigh the children's future lives with as much concern as they weigh their own, do they really love the children they beget? And can't the same question be asked of the addicted woman, the unloved woman, the unwed woman, or the woman who needs a baby inside her to feel alive? If we love a child for the child's sake, mustn't we be careful not to bring that child into the world until we can provide for the child the best possible environment of which we're capable?

I'm certainly not implying that a woman must never have a child simply because she is poor. Nor can I agree with the statement attributed to birth-control crusader Margaret Sanger by her critics, "More children from the fit, none from the unfit." For one thing, wealthy women already bear too many children.

Every woman has the *right* to have children, and there should be no compulsion in the field of sexual, marital or parenting relations, other than the prohibition of actions that have always been regarded as criminal, such as rape.

But this right should be exercised with responsibility. Responsible people seek to prepare themselves to have children long before they actually have them. Having a child and becoming a parent involves the most sacred of all responsibilities.

Delicate issues

I will admit that we have difficult and delicate trade-offs in this whole question of childbearing decisions. The argument that a woman should not have too many children — more than two, some might say — is countered by the insistence that there must not be any compulsion, direct or indirect. In the next chapter I will describe what I feel is a needed measure to discourage large families in the United States. Yet I would certainly not take AFDC payments or food stamps from any children that need them.

Still another delicate issue is that of abortion. Much as I would hope that sexual responsibility, backed up by effective contraception, will prevent unwanted pregnancies, we know that some such pregnancies will inevitably occur. For any woman who is pregnant and unmarried, the choice among options -- abortion, adoption, or single parenthood -- should be based not on what seems best for the woman, but on what's the most loving to the child. Usually single parenthood will be the least loving, even more cruel than abortion.

The role of government in the U.S. scene

It has often been pointed out that the economic position of America's elderly has improved dramatically since the 1960s because of liberalizations in social security and the enactment of Medicare. Meanwhile, the economic status of children has worsened, though mostly due to the increased proportion of single parent families. But whatever the cause, it is intolerable in a society as prosperous as ours that the economic status of children has not improved like the economic status of the elderly.

The political and religious right in our country insist that we have done far too much to "coddle" the poor. Rightists harp on the fact that after spending two trillion dollars in fighting poverty, we find the poor worse off than ever. They point out that more and more babies are born to unwed mothers, that school children are poorer than ever in math and English. That the cities are more crime-ridden and drug-infested than ever before. Their cure is to stop spending on the poor and to cut taxes further for the rich.

These critics are both right and wrong, right in the facts they mention, but wrong in their conclusions and in their proposed cure. There are millions of poor children in America, in small towns and rural areas as well as in the inner-cities, and we are spending far too little now on their support, health and education.

We can hope that we will not worsen this tragedy by continuing the irresponsible childbearing that has proliferated the children. But we have to resolve to do far more for the children already here. They are the victims, not the culprits, and to neglect them — as we have increasingly been doing — would victimize them still further. But not to neglect them takes money, and lots of it.

World Population Growth

We Americans have to rethink the matter of money. Where does our money go? Collectively, we spend billions for non-essentials. We pay entertainers and professional athletes salaries of a million dollars or more, not to mention what they get for endorsements, for which we ourselves are paying. Our legal system makes it possible for lawyers to obtain fees in the millions of dollars for individual civil or criminal cases.

We pay our leading business executives annual compensation of millions of dollars. Are they all worth it? How could some CEOs of American automobile companies be worth it, when they tried to sell cars to Japanese with steering-posts on the left rather than on the right? (Japanese drive on the left side of the street.) Would we have bought many Japanese cars with steering-posts on the right?

During 1994 we witnessed the Congressional fighting over the crime bill and the proposed health care reform bill. I am not going to argue the merits of the various bills. But were you aware of the millions of dollars in campaign contributions that lawmakers received from the National Rifle Association and the health insurance companies to influence legislation? Are you aware that much of this money really comes out of your own pockets?

I wonder whether even wealthy Americans believe that they are immune from the repercussions arising from the ever-increasing number of children living in poverty. They do not suffer from juvenile crime as much as the rest of us do, but they do suffer.

Government does have a tremendous role to play on behalf of America's children. Many in government are recognizing it. The National Commission on Children, recognizing that "the children are the poorest Americans", has proposed a system of tax credits, as already referred to, which will be discussed in the next chapter. For now, I want to discuss the major changes in U.S. tax policy, financing these credits would probably involve. The Commission proposed that they be paid for by increasing the basic tax rates for federal individual and corporate income tax, federal estate tax, and various excise taxes, as well as reallocation of part of present defense spending. I will refer only to individual income tax rates and to estate taxes.

Do We Love Our Children?

The Clinton deficit-reduction plan enacted in 1993 included higher marginal tax rates for high-income families. This was a partial reversal of Reaganomics. Prior to the 1981 tax revision, there was a 70 percent marginal rate at the highest income levels, but this was reduced first to 50 percent, then to 28 percent. The reduction to 28 percent was accompanied by the sacrifice of some tax shelters and the raising of the maximum capital gains tax rate from 25 percent to 28 percent. The maximum marginal rate was raised to 31 percent during the Bush administration. Under the Clinton plan, the maximum was raised to 39.6 percent for the portion of annual household income exceeding $1 million.

High as this 39.6 percent rate is, the Children's Commission proposals, or the alternatives I will suggest in the next chapter, may necessitate an even higher maximum marginal rate. If these proposals or alternatives ever come to the Congress, we will again hear predictions that high income tax rates on the very wealthy will discourage productivity and investment and have a negative economic effect — and possibly a reduction in tax revenue.

This last prediction has not been borne out with respect to the change to 39.6 percent. Recent Treasury data show increased income tax revenue. Why did the U.S. economy thrive as it did during the 1950s and 1960s, when the top marginal rate was 70 percent or higher? Admittedly, there were various tax shelters and loopholes then which are now closed. But even today there are large gifts to the very wealthy in our tax code. One of these is the mortgage interest deduction on mortgages as high as a million dollars. It reduces tax revenues by over $80 billion a year, most of the tax saving going to high-income households.

The top marginal income tax rates for several industrialized countries — among them France, Germany, Italy, the Netherlands, and Japan — are 50 percent or more, applying to incomes in excess of amounts corresponding to $300,000. Most of these countries have additional local taxes, some of them on income, just as we do. They also have excise taxes, value-added taxes, luxury taxes and much higher death-transfer taxes than we do. Moreover, a number of them have wealth taxes, levied against total personal assets. People in these countries do not like taxes any more than we would; however, they feel the benefits these taxes pay for are indispensable, and among these are generous benefits on behalf of their children. One of these benefits is excellent education; every one of these countries has more school days per year than ours (Japan's schools are 6 days a week) and pays their teachers accordingly.

Our entire economy clearly favors the very wealthy. Kevin Phillips and others write of the great concentration of wealth in the hands of the economic elite. In 1983 the wealthiest 0.5 percent of families owned 27 percent of the wealth. In 1980 (even before Reaganomics) the income distribution in the United States favored high-income families to a much greater degree than in other industrialized countries. The 1981 tax reduction bill that reduced income tax rates for the wealthy also greatly weakened the Federal estate tax, making it possible for increased inheritances by the very wealthy.

In the same years when leverage-buyouts of corporations were creating further concentration of economic power, at the same time producing millions of dollars in legal and brokerage fees, real earnings of many Americans were actually declining.

If U.S. society really loves its children, why cannot far more resources be devoted to their welfare, so that every child will have access to better education, better health care and nutrition? Why cannot our children live in a more equitable and egalitarian system, in which every child can be assured of the same opportunities and life prospects of the most fortunate children in our land?

In an earlier chapter, I also urged that our nation do far more than it now does for children in the LDCs. We now give about $15 billion a year in foreign aid — a smaller percentage of GNP than the foreign aid given by several European countries — but little of ours goes for the benefit of children. Of that $15 billion, almost half goes to only two countries, Israel and Egypt, more or less as a reward for their keeping at peace with each other.

Do We Love Our Children?

Ask yourself this question: "What possible benefit can there be to society for some families to enjoy after-tax incomes of hundreds of thousands or even millions of dollars, when many American children and far greater numbers of foreign children are so poverty-stricken as to lack adequate food and education and health care, and when some even lack a sheltered and safe place to sleep at night?"

Chapter 19

What We Can Do About Population Growth

"Whatsoever things are ... just"
— Paul (Philippians 4:8)

World population growth cannot be dramatically slowed unless the United States takes a leadership role far different from the mixed role that it has exhibited so far. The rest of the world thinks of us as a spoiled child who has everything he wants and still wants to deprive other children of their needs. One particular example of spoiled-child behavior has been our refusal to join other nations in agreeing to the International Law of the Sea, under which we would agree to preservation of the seabed and fair sharing of its products. (Our recent signing of the treaty has not yet been ratified by the Senate.)

In my work in the LDCs of Asia and Africa, I became very aware of the reaction of people there to the wastefulness of our life style. I referred in an earlier chapter to African views, however exaggerated, of American diet. In India and Sri Lanka, people I would meet on the street — even beggars — would reprimand us for our military expenditures, claiming that what we spend in a day for arms would feed millions of their hungry or cure millions of their sick.

An example of desired U.S. leadership

Are we willing to make sacrifices of the type that would be meaningful to people in high-fertility countries? Here is one that could be of real significance: Amend our Federal and state income tax laws by eliminating, or greatly reducing, the exemption for future-born (or future-conceived) children where a family already has two or more living children.

This step of revising our child exemptions under tax law would make it plain, both to ourselves and to the world, that we are not encouraging large families. At present, the amount of exemption per child ($2,450 as applied to taxes for the year 1994) is the same for a child in a one-child family and for each child in a large family. The tax effect of the exemption favors not only large families but also high-income families. A family whose income is in the 39.6 percent bracket gets a $970 saving per child, while a family in the 15 percent bracket gets only $368. A family whose income is too low to pay taxes obviously gets nothing from the exemption.

We could even have a higher exemption for the first child than for the second, knowing that it is the birth of the first child that often removes a mother from her job.

But if we wish not to encourage the birth of children in any family which already has two or more children, the best way is to deny any additional exemption for future-born, or future-conceived, children in such a family. This would not take away exemptions from children already born (or in gestation) when the change is enacted.

There is ample precedent for such a change in our present tax code. The child care credit now in effect provides the same amount for a second as for a first child, but there is no credit for an additional child. The earned-income credit available with respect to a single child is increased by only about five percent if there is a second child but not at all for a third or subsequent child.

There is also a limit in the maximum family benefit under social security which in effect limits the number of children who can get the full child's benefit.

What We Can Do

Even if no American woman were to bear a third or higher order child, we would in the short run still have more annual births than deaths. During 1991, 2.2 million Americans died, while 2.9 million women gave birth to their first or second child. But a marked reduction in the number of third or higher order births could rapidly reduce our annual natural increase.

Once the principle of limiting child exemptions so as not to encourage large families is agreed on, we can turn to the proposal of the National Commission on Children for refundable credits for each child. The Commission recommended a refundable credit of $1,000 for every American child. I would suggest consideration of the following steps:

1. Scale the credits according to the number of children, the first child's to be much more than $1,000, the second child's to be less than the first child's, with further reductions for other children, but none for future-born (or future-conceived) children of third or higher order.

2. Substitute the credits for tax exemptions.

3. Convert the credits to child's monthly allowances.

4. Include these allowances in taxable income. Treating the allowance payments as taxable income would add little if anything to the tax of a low-income family, but the tax paid by upper-income families would recoup some of the cost of the allowances.

Under my proposals, AFDC payments would still be available to families with more than two children and would be payable on a needs-test basis as now. But the total cost of AFDC would be cut substantially because child's allowances would be recognized as household income in determining a family's need.

The allowances could be scaled in such a way as to predetermine the net cost to the federal government of the new system. The effect of the proposals would be to increase subsidies to small and low-income families and to subject large families with high incomes to greater tax than at present. But the most conspicuous part of the proposed system would be to send out the message that large families are not to be encouraged, whether wealthy or poor.

This proposal is certain to arouse strong objections from both right and left in our country. From right, because new taxes will very likely be required. From left, because poor people are in effect encouraged to limit the size of their families. From pro-lifers, because more abortions might result.

This program does not compel, but only suggests, that we have small families. Society has the right to do at least this. For if society has an obligation of providing children's education, health care (at least in part), security and other benefits, then society has the right to set policy as to the number of children for whom it will provide.

Reduction of gasoline consumption

Except for a few oil-producing countries, the United States enjoys the lowest gasoline prices in the world. Raising gasoline prices through a greatly increased federal tax would reduce consumption, would greatly reduce pollution, and would raise revenue. It would reduce commuter driving by city dwellers and suburbanites. A portion of the increased federal revenue would be devoted to increased provision of public transportation.

Rural people and long-distance truckers would have the most justifiable complaint over increased gasoline costs. It may be possible that some plan could be worked out to relieve them. U.S. rural dwellers have far longer distances to travel than people in Europe or Asia, and the same is true of commercial transportation.

A question to be raised in this connection is: How do Australia and Canada make out with their much higher gasoline tax? Drivers and truckers in these countries have even greater distances to travel than we do.

Finally

There are many things which we as a nation can do to lessen world problems. A most important one is to stop the prolif-eration of armaments. During the cold war, it seemed necessary not only to engage in an arms race but also to supply arms to client states. But what is the point of that now? What is the purpose of the world powers' supplying arms to both India and Paki-stan so that they can war against each other, or to both Israel and Jordan?

What We Can Do

Why can't we, together with the help of countries like Britain, Germany, France and Japan, act to force lesser powers to disarm and to prevent them from ever getting new armaments?

The world's refugee crises affect not only the refugees but all of us in countries like our own. We suffer just from seeing the suffering that has taken place in 1994 in Bosnia, Rwanda and Haiti. If we take into our borders a few million refugees from these countries, we may relieve the plight of those few million, but we won't relieve the far greater plight of the many millions whom we don't take in. And we would also add greatly to our own urban problems, since almost all refugees go to the large cities.

So why can't we take prompt and decisive joint steps, even military steps when necessary, to stop the conflicts that convert peace-loving people into desperate refugees? No nation wants see any of its own armed personnel die in combat, but when we say this, we ignore the far greater number of deaths and other tragedies that have taken place in the countries just mentioned.

We can make the world safe for the world's children if we try hard enough to do so. The people of the world can insist that the world's resources be spent wisely instead of wastefully. They can insist that we stop polluting. That we disarm. And equally important, that we give more loving thought to the future welfare of our present children, and procreate future children only in such numbers that the world they will live in can give them the well-being, security and peace they will deserve.

We're at last giving overdue thought to making safe the physical environment for our children. Let's do the same for the human environment.

Demographic Appendix

This Appendix is included to acquaint you with the sources and nature of population data and to give you an added understanding of demographic relationships.

The majority of countries have periodic censuses in which they count their population. The United States is required by its Constitution to conduct a census every tenth year to determine the number of seats in the House of Representatives to which each State is entitled. The census also provides a wealth of population information used in government, business and research. The first census was in 1790, and the most recent was as of April 1, 1990.

In the 1990 census each household was asked seven questions about each of its individual members — each member's sex, age, marital status, etc. — and seven questions about the housing — type of building, number of rooms, etc. A sample of one household out of every six received a much longer questionnaire; it included questions on each member's education, citizenship, health, language, employment and income, and also additional questions about the household relating to such items as vehicles or utilities.

The Census Bureau also conducts censuses of business and agriculture and a variety of sample surveys. Among the surveys is the Current Population Survey, a monthly nationwide survey of a sample drawn from the total civilian population; this survey enables the Bureau to furnish useful estimates of the population and its characteristics during the ten-year intervals between censuses.

Next in importance to population censuses are tabulations of births, deaths and other vital events such as marriage and divorce. In the United States these data are derived from county and state records, and they are reported nationally by the National Center for Health Statistics. Some states did not have complete birth and death registration until the mid-1930s, so that rates for earlier years had to be partially estimated. Even today, some states do not report complete marriage and divorce data.

Most advanced countries have similar sets of demographic data, and even the majority of developing countries have censuses.

171

World Population Growth

Basic demographic rates

The rates most commonly used in describing the demography of a country or an area or an ethnic group are: (1) the crude death rate, (2) the crude birth rate, (3) the natural increase rate, and (4) the infant mortality rate. Another commonly used term is "life expectancy", to be described later.

The crude death rate of an area (etc.) is the number of deaths in the area in a year per 1,000 population in that year. Usually, the population base is taken as the mean population in that year, or the population in the middle of the year. For example, if the U.S. population on July 1, 1990, were 250 million and there were 2.25 million deaths in 1990, the crude death rate would be 9 per 1,000, or simply 9.

Similarly, if there were 4.0 million babies born alive in 1990 (with 250 million population), the crude birth rate would be 16.

The natural increase rate is the excess of the crude birth rate of a year over the crude death rate. Usually it is expressed as a percent instead of per 1,000. Thus with a crude birth rate of 16 and a crude death rate of 9, the natural increase rate would be 0.7 percent, rather than 7 or 7 per thousand.

When we use the term natural increase, we mean the increase (or decrease) due only to births less deaths, not the additional increase or decrease from immigration or emigration.

The infant mortality rate is the number of infant deaths in a year (deaths of babies occurring before their first birthday) per 1,000 births in the year; births mean babies born alive (not stillborn). If there are 4.0 million babies born in a year, and 36 thousand babies die in the year before reaching their first birthday, the infant mortality rate is 9. Note that babies who die in the current year before reaching their first birthday may have been born in the preceding year; those born this year who die next year before reaching their first birthday will be counted in figuring next year's infant mortality rate.

The four rates defined above are very commonly used, but to have a satisfactory quantitative understanding of both mortality (deaths) and fertility (births), we should examine more analytical measures.

Demographic Appendix

The life table

As you know, the probability of a person's death in a year depends considerably on the person's age. The probability of death in the first year of life is essentially the same as the infant mortality rate. In the United States this rate in 1990 was 9.1 deaths per 1,000 births (about 10 for males, 8 for females). At subsequent childhood ages, however, the annual probability of death was much less than 9. It was at its minimum at age 10 (about 0.2 deaths per 1,000), and then gradually rose age by age, not reaching 9 per 1,000 again until about age 50 for men and about age 60 for women.

The following is an excerpt from a life table prepared by the Social Security Administration and representing the mortality of U.S. females in the year 1990. Like most life tables, what this life table is saying is as follows: We start out with a hypothetical 100,000 newborn females (age 0) and apply the infant death rate, which for females is .00827; this results in 827 of the 100,000 dying at age 0, leaving 99,173 alive on their first birthday(age 1). To these 99,173 we apply the age 1 death probability of .00065, which results in 64 deaths at age 1, leaving 99,109 alive on their second birthday (age 2), and so on. The table starts out like this:

Age	Number living	Probability of dying	Number dying
0	100,000	.00827	827
1	99,173	.00065	64
2	99,109	.00042	42
3	99,067	.00031	31

The U.S. male probability of death for every age exceeds the female probability. (This was not always true in the past, nor is it true even now in many developing countries.)

Using the complete table, it is possible to show the number of persons living in each 5-year age group in the female population, assuming that 100,000 females are born each year, that for each age the death probabilities continue without change, and there is no immigration or emigration. The results look like the table on the following page.

World Population Growth

Age group	Alive at entry into age group	Living within age group (000)	% of total pop.	Living at this and all older ages (000)	Life expectancy at beg. of age group (years)
0-4	100,000	495.6	6.30%	7,865	78.65
5-9	99,013	494.9	6.29	7,369	74.43
10-14	98,920	494.4	6.28	6,874	69.49
15-19	98,824	493.5	6.27	6,380	64.56
20-24	98,592	492.3	6.26	5,886	59.70
25-29	98,324	490.9	6.24	5,394	54.86
30-34	98,006	489.0	6.22	4,903	50.03
35-39	97,588	486.6	6.19	4,414	45.23
40-44	97,027	483.3	6.15	3,928	40.48
45-49	96,225	477.9	6.08	3,444	35.79
50-54	94,973	470.5	5.98	2,966	31.23
55-59	92,945	457.4	5.82	2,496	26.85
60-64	89,826	438.0	5.57	2,038	22.69
65-69	85,074	409.2	5.20	1,600	18.81
70-74	78,204	368.6	4.69	1,191	15.23
75-79	68,790	313.8	3.99	823	11.96
80-84	56,215	242.8	3.09	509	9.05
85+	40,391	266.1	3.38	266	6.59
Totals		7,864.8	100.00%		

Much of the above table will be self-explanatory, but you should note that the numbers in the second column from the right are obtained by summing, from the bottom up, the numbers in the second column from the left. The top number, 7,865 thousand, therefore represents the total female population. The life expectancies are found by dividing the numbers in the column second from the right by the numbers alive in the first column. Thus the life expectancy at birth, 78.65 years, is 7,865 thousand divided by 100,000, the number of females born each year.

Demographic Appendix

The population represented by a life table is called a stationary population, and the number of females dying each year is 100,000, the same as the number born. Therefore the crude death rate as well as the crude birth rate is 100,000 divided by 7,865 thousand, or 12.71 (per 1,000), and the life expectancy at birth is the reciprocal of the crude death (or birth) rate. The life expectancy at birth is also equal to the average age at death. At any age greater than 0, the life expectancy is the number of years of future lifetime for those alive at that age.

Life expectancy at birth is perhaps the most satisfactory measure for comparing one country's mortality with that of another, or for comparing mortality over different periods of time. The estimated U.S. life expectancy in 1994 is about 76 in total, about 72.5 for males, 79.5 for females. For white and Asian-American populations the values are slightly higher, for blacks several points lower, for black females 75, for black males only 65. Life expectancy has improved considerably over this century. The U.S. life expectancy in 1900 was 49 in total, 48 for males, 50 for females.

For Mexico in 1994 the estimated life expectancy is about 70 in total, for Canada and most northern European countries one or two points higher than the U.S., for sub-Saharan Africa mostly about 50.

Crude death rates are often an unsatisfactory measure of comparison between countries. The U.S. crude death rate is now about 9. Because of its much younger population, Mexico's crude death rate is only about 6, even though at every age Mexico's mortality is somewhat higher than ours.

Note that in the above stationary population, females at ages 65 and over are 20.3% of the total female population. In the actual 1990 U.S. population, females 65 and over are only 14.7% of total females, and males 65 and over are 10.4% of total males. In Chapter 14, it was noted that if there were no immigration and if fertility remained at replacement level, the U.S. population would become older in composition. In the long run, it would have the same age distribution as the life table.

World Population Growth

Fertility rates

Earlier we defined the crude birth rate, which relates the number of births to the total population. More pertinent, however, are "fertility rates", which relate births to the number of women of childbearing age. The following table shows age-specific fertility rates for the US for 5-year periods since 1925 and arranged in 5-year age groups. These rates are partly estimated, since birth registration was not complete during the early 1930s.

ASFRs in the years indicated

Ages	1925 -29	1930 -34	1935 -39	1940 -44	1945 -49	1950 -54	1955 -59	1960 -64	1965 -69	1970 -74	1975 -79	1980 -84	1985 -89	1990
10-14	*	*	*	*	*	*	*	*	.001	.001	.001	.001	.001	.001
15-19	.051	.046	.048	.058	.072	.089	.094	.083	.069	.063	.059	.053	.053	.060
20-24	.131	.117	.119	.152	.186	.219	.255	.240	.177	.137	.112	.115	.110	.118
25-29	.127	.112	.108	.136	.159	.179	.196	.190	.147	.124	.109	.113	.111	.120
30-34	.099	.080	.074	.092	.105	.111	.117	.108	.081	.062	.056	.062	.072	.081
35-39	.065	.050	.044	.050	.057	.055	.059	.053	.039	.026	.019	.020	.026	.032
40-44	.025	.020	.016	.015	.017	.016	.017	.016	.011	.007	.004	.004	.004	.005
45-49	.003	.002	.002	.002	.001	.001	.001	.001	*	*	*	*	*	*
TFR	2.51	2.14	2.06	2.53	2.99	3.35	3.69	3.45	2.62	2.10	1.80	1.84	1.88	2.08

*=rate less than .0005

Each age-specific rate is the composite rate for its particular age group. In 1990 the rate for the age-group 15-19 is shown as 060, but it is obvious the rate for age 15 is less than .060 and the rate for age 19 greater than .060. Also, each rate is a composite for all marital status; all women of the given age are included in the denominator and all births in the numerator, regardless of marital status. In 1990, 74 percent of the births for ages under 20, and 39 percent for ages 20-24, were births to unmarried women.

The most significant measure of fertility is the "total fertility rate" (TFR). Since there are five ages in each age group, the TFR for any period is five times the sum of the ASFRs. Thus for 1980-84 the TFR is 1.84, five times the sum .368 in the 1980-84 column. The TFR for a given period indicates the total number of children born to a woman if she were to survive to age 50 and if at each age she were to experience the fertility rates for that period.

Demographic Appendix

You will see that the maximum TFR of 3.69 was in 1955-59, the height of the "baby boom". The lowest was 1.80 for 1975-79, but the depression years 1935-39 had a low of 2.06. Note that at ages under 30, the ASFRs of the 1980's were little different from those of the 1930's, though much lower than in the baby-boom years. For older ages, the rates during 1975-79 were considerably lower than at any earlier period, but rose again in the late 1980's and into 1990, as many women were marrying later and were bearing children after 30 instead of at an earlier age. The increasing proportion of Mexican-born women in the population is also a factor in the recent fertility increases.

Replacement level — and the effect of age distribution

A set of fertility rates is said to be at "replacement-level" if a continuation of these rates without change and in conjunction with mortality (or survival) rates, also continuing without change, will eventually produce a stationary population. The fertility rates shown above for 1990 produce a TFR of 2.08, and in combination with the 1990 life table, they closely represent replacement level. The following figures demonstrate this, producing approximately the life table starting point of 100,000 births.

Age group	Female pop. (000)	Fertility rate	Product = annual births (000)
10-14	494.4	.001	0.5
15-19	493.5	.060	29.6
20-24	492.3	.118	58.1
25-29	490.9	.120	58.9
30-34	489.0	.081	39.6
35-39	486.6	.032	15.6
40-44	483.3	.005	2.4

Total births	204.7
Female births	99.9
(48.78% of total)	

World Population Growth

The 1990 U.S. census showed a total female population of 127,470 thousand, 16.207 times the life table female population of 7,865 thousand. Consider two female populations of 127,470 thousand each. One has the figures in the above table multiplied by 16.207, a stationary population with the same age composition as the life table population. The other is the census population. Applying these ASFRs to each population, we get these results:

Age group	Fertility rate	Stationary population Number (000)	Births (000)	Census population Number (000)	Births (000)
10-14	.001	8,017	8.0	8,347	8.3
15-19	.060	7,998	479.9	8,651	519.1
20-24	.118	7,979	941.5	9,345	1,102.7
25-29	.120	7,956	954.7	10,617	1,274.0
30-34	.081	7,925	641.9	10,986	889.9
35-39	.032	7,886	252.4	10,061	321.9
40-44	.005	7,833	39.2	8,924	44.6

Ages 10-44 totals   55,594   3,317.6   66,931   4,160.5 *

* Actual numbers: 1990   4,158.2
                    1991   4,110.9

Both populations are the same in total number, but the number of women of childbearing age in the actual population is much greater than in the life table population, because of both high fertility of past years and high immigration of recent years. As the result, the high level of present births will keep the U.S. population growing for some decades even with a TFR no greater than replacement level, and would do so even if there were no further immigration.

It is at the older ages, especially from 65 on, that the life table population greatly exceeds the census population.

Demographic Appendix

Replacement-level fertility in general

If there were no mortality before or during the childbearing ages, and if exactly half the babies born were female, replacement- level fertility would require a TFR of only 2.0. In the United States, with current mortality, only 48.8% of newborn babies are female, and about 2% of them fail to survive into mid-childbearing ages, and so a TFR of about 2.1 is required for replacement-level fertility. The same requirement would apply to Canada, Australia and most of Europe. Because of somewhat higher mortality, a TFR of about 2.2 would be needed in Mexico, about 2.4 in India, and even higher TFRs in some African countries, up to a maximum of about 3.2.

Population projection

To project a population whose present size and sex-and-age composition is known, we must first be able to make assumptions as to rates of mortality, fertility and migration. For purposes of illustration, we will project the 1990 U.S. female population and make the assumption that the 1990 life table and 1990 fertility rates continue in effect. In this illustration, we will assume no net immigration or emigration. Since we have data in 5-year age groups, we will find it easiest to project 5 years at a time.

To start with, we apply an appropriate survival ratio to the number living in each 5-year age group in 1990 to find the number living at the next older age group in 1995. Suppose we choose the age group 15-19, which included 8651 thousand females. The life table number living at 15-19 is 493.5, and living at 20-24 is 492.3. Since dividing 492.3 by 493.5 gives the survival ratio is .9974, we can apply this ratio to the 8651 thousand living at ages 15-19 in 1990, and obtain 8629 thousand living at ages 20-24 in 1995. Similarly we can obtain the numbers living in 1995 at all ages 5-84.

The ratio of the life-table population 85 and over (266.1 thousand) to the population 80 and over (508.9 thousand) is .5229, and this ratio is applied to the 1990 census population at ages 80 and over to obtain the 1995 population at ages 85 and over.

World Population Growth

To obtain the number living at ages 0-4 in 1995, however, we must calculate the births occurring from April 1990 to March 1995. The procedure is the same as in the previous calculation of births, except that here we apply the appropriate fertility rates to the mean of the numbers living at these two dates. The number living in 1990 at ages 20-24 was 9345 thousand and the mean of that number and the 8629 thousand we have already calculated for ages 20-24 in 1995 is 8,987 thousand. We then apply the age 20-24 fertility rate of .118 to this mean, and we get an average of 1060.5 thousand annual births to women 20-24 during the period April 1990 to April 1995. We do the same for all age groups from 10-14 to 40-44, and multiply the sum of the resulting births by 5 to obtain the total births in the 5-year period.

Ages	Living 1990 (000)	Survival ratio	Living 1995 (000)	Mean no. living (000)	Fertility rate	Annual births (000)
10-14	8,347	.9990	8,828	8,588	.001	8.6
15-19	8,651	.9983	8,333	8,492	.060	509.5
20-24	9,345	.9974	8,629	8,987	.118	1,060.5
25-29	10,617	.9963	9,310	9,964	.120	1,195.7
30-34	10,986	.9950	10,564	10,775	.081	872.8
35-39	10,061	.9932	10,911	10,486	.032	335.6
40-44	8,924	.9901	9,961	9,442	.005	47.2

Average annual births during 1990-95   4,029.9

We now multiply the result by .4878 to obtain the number of female births, multiply that result by .9912 to deduct the deaths under age 5 during the 5-year period, and then multiply by five to obtain the number of females living at age 0-4 in 1995. The result is:

4029.9 * .4878 * .9912 * 5 = 9,742 (thousand)

Demographic Appendix

This procedure has been used to project the U.S. female census population for every fifth year from 1990 to the year 2100, and the results for selected years are shown below. All these results, of course, assume the continuation of 1990 fertility and mortality, and, most important, no net immigration. Remember too that the 1990 census undercounted the actual population.

Projection of the U.S. female census population

Age group	Living 1990	Living 1995	Living 2000	Living 2030	Living 2035	Living 2100
		(all population numbers are thousands)				
0-4	8962	9742	9173	9029	8953	8967
5-9	8837	8949	9728	9127	9016	8954
10-14	8347	8828	8941	9133	9118	8950
15-19	8651	8333	8813	8969	9117	8946
20-24	9345	8629	8311	8756	8945	8935
25-29	10617	9310	8597	8739	8724	8903
30-34	10986	10564	9264	9033	8695	8847
35-39	10061	10911	10492	9528	8972	8779
40-44	8924	9961	10803	8678	9433	8707
45-49	7060	8815	9840	8464	8572	8634
50-54	5836	6950	8675	7876	8330	8518
55-59	5497	5674	6757	7949	7657	8258
60-64	5669	5264	5433	8244	7612	7859
65-69	5579	5296	4918	8783	7702	7329
70-74	4596	5026	4771	8228	7911	6659
75-79	3722	3904	4278	6458	7004	5738
80-84	2567	2880	3021	4476	4997	4447
85+	2222	2504	2815	3599	4223	4775

Totals
	127470	131540	134629	145071	144983	142206

World Population Growth

Corresponding to the 2030 female population of 145 million would be a male population of 140 million, a total of 285 million. You will note that the increase in the total population becomes less rapid with the passage of time. For individual age groups, there are both increases and decreases, largely due to the irregular age distribution of the 1990 population. Over a long period of time the age distribution will smooth out as will the progression for each age group.

Moreover, by the year 2030 the total population will have reached its peak. Thereafter there will be a slow decline, due to TFR being very slightly below replacement level. This is exactly what the U.S. population would do without immigration or emigration and with continuation of constant fertility and mortality rates.

One further thing you should note is that ultimately the age distribution of the population becomes almost the same as that of the life-table (or stationary) population, which you may verify for yourself from the 2100 column. (It would be exactly the same if TFR were exactly replacement level.)

Again, you must note that this projection has been an exercise in that it has assumed no net immigration. All realistic assumptions do include considerable immigration, and the Census Bureau's most recent projections include greater immigration than before, as well as high fertility of immigrant women. Under these projections, U.S. population may pass 400 million in the coming century.

Projection of Mexico's population

The above projection of the U.S. female population shows a 14 percent growth over 40 years even though fertility has been below replacement level since about 1972. China's effort to limit family size has reduced fertility well below replacement level, but its population is still growing by about 1.1 percent a year. For an LDC such as Mexico with fertility still above replacement level, a momentum has been generated which will prolong population growth for a long period, even after its TFR falls below replacement level.

Demographic Appendix

Mexico's TFR in the 1960s was about 6. In 1990 it had dropped to 3.6 and it is about 3.2 now. Because of the very high fertility of past decades, its age distribution is such that births would well exceed deaths even if it had only replacement-level fertility now.

Two projections have been made of the Mexican female population, starting with the year 1990, in the same manner as the above U.S. projection. In the first of the Mexican projections, it was assumed that the estimated Mexican mortality and fertility rates in effect in 1990 would continue indefinitely. The survival rates used were drawn from a female life table with 70 years life expectancy at birth, and the fertility rates produced a TFR of 3.6. In the second of the projections, the same survival rates were used, but the fertility rates were reduced by approximately 38 percent, producing a TFR of about 2.2, which should be replacement-level fertility corresponding to the mortality assumption made.

The first projection resulted in a population increasing in the long run by about 10.3 percent every five years, not quite 2.0 percent annually. If these mortality and fertility rates were to continue without change, and without emigration, the female population would reach 146 million in the year 2050, and the total population (male plus female) would be about 290 million, exceeding what the U.S. population would then be without immigration. With this first projection, the Mexican population would still be a very young one, with over 35 percent of its people under age 15.

The second projection, which assumed replacement-level fertility starting in 1990, showed Mexico's total female population growing from 42.3 million in 1990 to 70.0 million in 2055 before leveling off, a 65 percent increase in 65 years. Totals for every fifth year follows.

World Population Growth

Mexican female population in millions assuming replacement-level beginning in 1990

1990	42.3	2015	58.1	2040	67.8
1995	45.2	2020	60.7	2045	68.7
2000	48.4	2025	62.9	2050	69.5
2005	51.8	2030	64.8	2055	70.0
2010	55.2	2035	66.5	2060	70.0

A total of 70 million females would mean a total of 140 million for both males and females. Most estimates reach higher totals than that, since it will probably take a few decades before fertility is down to replacement level. If Mexican fertility drops to replacement level by the year 2010 and then continues to decline further, and if considerable emigration also continues, Mexico's population might top out in the range of 150 to 160 million about the year 2050.

This sort of growth is fairly typical of what may happen in many LDCs. Their high fertility of the recent past has created a growth momentum such that population may grow by 50 percent or more even after fertility is brought down to replacement level.

Order Form

To order additional copies of:

World Population Growth

please send $14.95 plus $2.50
Shipping & Handling,
Washington residents please include 8.2% sales tax. Make
check or money order payable to:
Peanut Butter Publishing
226 2nd Ave W.
Seattle, WA 98119
(206) 281-5965

If you prefer to use VISA or Mastercard, please fill in your
card's number and expiration date. Please circle appropriate
card.

□ □ □ □ □ □ □ □ □ □ □ □ □ □ □ □

Signature_____

exp. date_____

_____Copies @ $14.95 ea._____

$2.50 Shipping & Handling_____

Washington State residents add 8.2%_____

Total enclosed_____

Name_____

Address_____

City, State, Zip_____

Please list additional copies to be sent to other
addresses on a separate sheet.